THE AMERICAN PEOPLE

- O *The Native American People of the East*
- O *The Native American People of the West*
- O *The American People in Colonial New England*
- ● *The American People in the Colonial South*
- O *The American People in the Antebellum North*
- O *The American People in the Antebellum South*
- O *The American People on the Western Frontier*
- O *The American People in the Industrial City*
- O *The American People in the Depression*
- O *The American People in the Age of Kennedy*

```
F     Axtell, James L
212
.A97   The American
       people in the
       colonial South
```

DATE DUE			
DEC 12 1989			
AUG 24 1993			
AUG 18 1998			

DISCARD

SOUTH CAMPUS LIBRARY
Community College of Allegheny County
West Mifflin, Pennsylvania 15122

The American People In the Colonial South

Edited by
JAMES AXTELL

P
Pendulum Press, Inc.

West Haven, Connecticut

COPYRIGHT © 1973 BY PENDULUM PRESS, INC.
All Rights Reserved

Clothbound Edition ISBN 0-88301-082-8 Complete Set
0-88301-086-0 This Volume

Paperback Edition ISBN 0-88301-066-6 Complete Set
0-88301-070-4 This Volume

Library of Congress Catalog Card Number. 72-95868

Published by
Pendulum Press, Inc.
The Academic Building
Saw Mill Road
West Haven, Connecticut 06516

Printed in the United States of America

Cover Design by Dick Brassil, Silverman Design Group
Cover Print Courtesy The Bettmann Archive

CONTENTS

	Introduction	13
I.	Birth	15
II.	Growth	39
III.	Love and Marriage	107
IV.	Right and Wrong	125
V.	Heaven and Earth	157
VI.	Death	179

ABOUT THE EDITOR

James Axtell, the recipient of a B.A. degree from Yale University and a Ph.D. from Cambridge University, has also studied at Oxford University and was a postdoctoral fellow at Harvard University. Mr. Axtell has taught history at Yale and is currently Associate Professor of Anglo-American History at Sarah Lawrence College. He is on the editorial board of *History of Education Quarterly* and has been a consultant to the American Council of Learned Societies. He has published several articles and reviews and is the author of a forthcoming book, *The School upon a Hill: Education and Society in Colonial New England.*

ACKNOWLEDGMENTS

Grateful acknowledgment is made to the authors and publishers who granted permission to reprint the following selections:

American Husbandry, edited by Harry J. Carmen, reprinted by permission of Columbia University Press.

Bases of the Plantation Society, edited by Aubrey C. Land, reprinted by permission of Harper and Company.

The Carolina Backcountry on the Eve of Revolution: The Journal and Other Writings of Charles Woodmason, Anglican Itinerant, edited by Richard J. Hooker, reprinted by permission of Institute of Early American History and Culture.

"County Court Records of Accomack-Northampton, Virginia, 1632-1640," edited by Susie M. Ames, reprinted by permission of *The American Historical Review*.

The Diary of Colonel Landon Carter of Sabine Hall, 1752-1778, edited by Jack P. Greene, reprinted by permission of University Press of Virginia.

Documentary History of American Industrial Society, edited by Ulrich B. Phillips. Published by Russell and Russell.

The Journal of John Harrower: An Indentured Servant in the Colony of Virginia, 1773-1776, edited by Edward Miles Riley, reprinted by permission of University Press of Virginia and Colonial Williamsburg.

Journals and Letters of Philip Vickers Fithian, 1773-1774: A Plantation Tutor of the Old Dominion, edited by Hunter, Dickenson and Farish, reprinted by permission of University Press of Virginia and Colonial Williamsburg.

Narratives of Early Virginia, edited by Lyon Gardiner, published by Barnes and Noble.

William Fitzhugh and His Chesapeake World 1676-1701, edited by Richard Beale Davis, reprinted by permission of University of North Carolina Press and Virginia Historical Society.

FOREWORD

The American People is founded on the belief that the study of history in the schools and junior levels of college generally begins at the wrong end. It usually begins with abstract and pre-digested *conclusions*—the conclusions of other historians as filtered through the pen of a textbook writer—and not with the primary sources of the past and unanswered *questions*—the starting place of the historian himself.

Since we all need, use, and think about the past in our daily lives, we are all historians. The question is whether we can be skillful, accurate, and useful historians. The only way to become such is to exercise our historical skills and interests until we gain competence. But we have to exercise them in the same ways the best historians do or we will be kidding ourselves that we are *doing* history when in fact we are only absorbing sponge-like the results of someone else's historical competence.

Historical competence must begin with one crucial skill—the ability to distinguish between past and present. Without a sharp sense of the past as a different time from our own, we will be unable to accord the people of the past the respect that we would like to receive from the people of the future. And without according them that respect, we will be unable to recognize their integrity as individuals or to understand them as human beings.

A good sense of the past depends primarily on a good sense of the present, on experience, and on the imaginative empathy to relate ourselves to human situations not our own. Although most students have had a relatively brief experience of life and have not yet given full expression to their imaginative sympathies, they do possess the one essential prerequisite for the study of history—the lives they have lived from birth to young adulthood. This should be the initial focus of their study of the past, not remotely adult experiences to which they cannot yet relate, such as politics, diplomacy, and war.

Thus the organizing perspective of this series is the universal life experiences that all people have: being born, growing up, loving and marrying, working and playing, behaving and misbehaving, worshipping, and dying. As only he could, Shakespeare portrayed these cycles in *As You Like It* (Act II, scene vii):

>All the world's a stage,
>And all the men and women merely players.
>They have their exits and their entrances;
>And one man in his time plays many parts,
>His acts being seven ages. At first the infant,
>Mewling and puking in the nurse's arms.
>And then the whining school-boy, with his satchel
>And shining morning face, creeping like snail
>Unwillingly to school. And then the lover,
>Sighing like furnace, with a woeful ballad
>Made to his mistress' eyebrow. Then a soldier,
>Full of strange oaths, and bearded like a pard;
>Jealous in honour sudden and quick in quarrel,
>Seeking the bubble reputation
>Even in the cannon's mouth. And then the justice,
>In fair round belly with good capon lined,
>With eyes severe and beard of formal cut,
>Full of wise saws and modern instances;
>And so he plays his part. The sixth age shifts
>Into the lean and slipper'd pantaloon,
>With spectacles on nose and pouch on side;
>His youthful hose, well saved, a world too wide
>For his shrunk shank; and his big manly voice,
>Turning again toward childish treble, pipes
>And whistles in his sound. Last scene of all,
>That ends this strange eventful history,
>Is second childishness, and mere oblivion,
>Sans teeth, sans eyes, sans taste, sans everything.

These are experiences to which any student can relate and from which he can learn, simply because they surround him daily in his home, community, and not least, school.

There is an additional reason for focussing on the universal life cycle. If history is everything that happened in the past, obviously some things were and are more important than others. Until fairly recently the things historians have found important have been the turning points or *changes* in history—"great" men and "great" events. But recently, with the help of anthropologists, historians have come to a greater awareness of the importance of stability and inertia, of *non*-change in society. For every society—and therefore its history—is a mixture of change and stability, of generally long periods of fixity punctuated now and then by moments of modification and change.

The major reason for the stability of society is the conservative bent of human behavior and ideals, the desire to preserve, hold, fix, and keep stable. People acquire habits and habits impede change. The habits people acquire are the common ways the members of a society react to the world—how they behave and feel and think in common—which distinguish them from other societies and cultures. So at bottom history is about ordinary people, how they did things alike and together that gave continuity and durability to their society so that it could change to meet new circumstances without completely losing its former identity and character.

America is such a society and *The American People* is an attempt to provide representative selections from primary sources about the lives and habits of ordinary people in periods of history that are usually known in textbooks for their great changes.

Since the experience of each student is the only prerequisite for the study of primary sources at the first level, annotations and introductory material have been reduced to a minimum, simply enough to identify the sources, their authors, and the circumstances in which they were written.

But the remains of the past are mute by themselves. Many sources have survived that can tell us what happened in the past and why, but they have to be questioned properly to reveal their secrets. So by way of illustration, a number of questions have been asked in each chapter, but these should be supplemented by the students whose experiences and knowledge and interests are, after all, the flywheel of the educational process. Although the questions and sources are divided into chapters, they should be used freely in the other chapters; the collection should be treated as a whole. And although most of the illustrative questions are confined to the sources at hand, questions that extend to the present should be asked to anchor the acquired knowledge of the past in the immediate experience of the present. Only then will learning be real and lasting and history brought to life.

INTRODUCTION

Like a field of hardy tobacco, the colonial South ripened slowly. From its inauspicious beginnings at Jamestown in 1607, the Virginia colony grew from a hundred men and four boys—a characteristically male population in that commercial colony—to 8000 souls in 1640, 15,000 in 1649, and an estimated 40,000 by 1666. In all, some 80,000 Englishmen found their way to the Chesapeake region between 1630 and 1700, half of them in the third quarter of the century when England experienced a series of severe crop failures. Most of them, perhaps as many as three-fourths, arrived under some form of indentured bondage, under contract for a specified number of years to an employer who had paid their passage to America.

But Englishmen and Indians were not the only inhabitants of the colonial South. In 1619 a Dutch man-of-war brought a new cargo to Virginia that was to alter irrevocably the economic and social condition of the south. As if they were any other form of merchandise or chattel, "twenty Negars" were traded to the leaders of the Virginia Company for "victualles" for the ship's crew. The frenzied importation of slaves that characterized the 18th century did not begin immediately, however. Until 1660 only 20 slaves entered the colony annually and in the last four decades of the century less than 90 annually. By 1700 Virginia's black population stood at an estimated 8000 persons. Large-scale importation of perpetually bonded labor had to wait for the success of rice culture after 1690 and indigo culture after 1740 in the Carolinas. Thus in the first century of the colonial south the heavy labor of clearing woods, draining swamps, building houses and barns, and cultivating crops was done primarily by white hands, those of predominately small farmers of estates less than £100 and indentured servants.

Unfortunately, the "little people" who comprised about 95 percent of the southern population were not given to making or preserving written accounts of their daily lives. Many if not most were barely literate and too busy or too tired at the end of the day to record thoughts and actions. The texture of their lives, when it can be seen at all, must be recaptured at second hand from the records of the colonial leaders who saw them in neighboring fields, the marketplace, and the courts. But mostly they are invisible or darkly reflected in the well-recorded history of the upper economic class, the great commercial planters whose slaves and wealth freed their hands and heads for the more literate work of diaries, account books, and letters. It is these men and their families who cast the tallest shadows over our image of the colonial South—a fact well worth remembering in the pages that follow.

I. BIRTH

Childrearing practices change very little over time, as many a reformer has discovered to his chagrin. Who were regarded as the authorities in medicine? Why were infants swaddled? For how long? What were the dangers of it? What was the state of Physiology in the 17th century? What, when, by whom, and how were infants fed? Why and for how long was the mother forbidden to breastfeed her new-born infant? What were the dangers of using wet-nurses? What reasons did English mothers give for not nursing their own infants? Where were infants supposed to be changed and washed? What does this say about the living conditions in English homes of the day? Was the doctor more fastidious about his patients than their parents were? When and how were children weaned? What was the first religious duty of the father of a newborn child? Why was the penalty for concealing the birth of a bastard child so harsh? Did the gentry practice contraception? Were men privy to the intimate events of birth? How knowledgeable were gentry women about child-bearing?

Most of the settlers of the southern colonies were English, so naturally their childbearing practices were largely reproductions of English examples. Jacques Guillemeau (1550-1613), chirurgeon to the French king, wrote the most popular handbook on the delivery and care of children in 17th-century Europe. Child-Birth; or, The Happy Deliverie of Women *was translated from the French original many times for English readers, and thus served as both a survey of the accepted practices of the day and the most advanced obstetrical advice to be had. The following passages occur on pp. 10-27 of the short treatise entitled* The Nursing of Children *which was appended to the 1612 London edition of* Child-Birth.

The care which a Nurse must have of all the parts of the childs body.

CHAP. III.

The nurse should be chosen a month or two before the woman be delivered, that she may alwaies have an eye over her, and her child, and then as soone as the Woman shall bee brought abed, and that the childe hath passed through the hands of the Midwife, or keeper, and is swathed by them he shall be delivered to the nurse to give him sucke, and have a care of him . . .

How the Nurse must shift the child.

CHAP. IIII.

We must not onely have a regard, to such defects of Nature, as the child may bring with him from his mothers wombe, and cure them: but we must also looke, and have an eye, that the Nurse, or shee that swathes, and dresseth him, doe not make him worse: and of a well fashioned child, in all the parts of his body, do not make him deformed or mishapen, and so spoile him. For in swathing the child, most commonly they bind and crush him so hard, that they make him grow crooked. Some swath all the childs body hard to make him have a goodly necke, and to make him seeme the fatter: but this crushing makes his brest and the ribs which are fastned to the back-bone, to stand out; so that they are bended, and draw the *vertebre* to them, which makes the backe bone, to bend and give out eyther inwardly, or outwardly, or else on the one side: and that causeth the childe to be eyther crump-shouldred, or crooked brested, or else to have one of his shoulders stand farther out then the other, some also bind the hips so hard that they become very smal, and that hinders them from growing and waxing big. Which doth much harme, especially to maids, who should have large hips, that when they come to age, they may bring foorth goodly children.

Galen hath observed, that the too straight and hard binding or crushing of the hams, and legges of little children, when they are swathed, doth make them grow crooked legged and they will remaine, as the Latines call it *Vari* or *Valgi*; going either inward or outward with their knees. This imperfection may also happen through the Nurses fault, by carrying the childe alwaies upon one arme, and the same side: and by holding the childs knees hard towards her, making them stand like a bow: For the preventing of which mischances, the Nurses shall carry their children, sometimes on the right side, and sometimes on the left. And they must likewise swath them, but loosely, stretching downe their armes, all along their sides, without binding or crushing them hard together.

Of the childs cradle, and how it is to be placed; and also how the child ought to be laide when he goes to sleepe.

Chap. V.

When the child shall bee thus dressed, and swathed, it will then be fit to let him sleepe and take some rest, for which purpose he must be laid in his cradle: fitted with a little mattresse, which shall be laid deepe to the bottome, that the sides of the cradle may be a great deale above the mattresse; that so the childe may as it were sinke downe in his cradle for feare least he fall out of it. Then upon the Mattresse shal be laid a pillow, that is somwhat soft, to lay the childe upon, letting him lye the first month upon his backe: but afterwards when hee is waxed a little bigger let him lye sometimes on his right side, and sometimes on the left, having his head a little raised up, that the excrements of his braine may the more easily flow and passe through the emunctoryes thereof: And hee must bee bound and tyed in with strings, least in rocking him, he fall out of his Cradle. At the head of the Cradle let there bee a little Arch made of wood, or Ozier to lay a coverlet over it, thereby to keepe away the wind, and that no dust fall upon him. But it would be more convenient (for those that can fitly have it) to set the Cradle within a little bed, the Curteynes drawne round about it.

Now, concerning the place where the Cradle must stand, it will be verie fit, that it be in a chamber that is neither too light, nor to darke, nor too hote, nor too cold: For if it be too light, it spends the spirits of the sight, and hindreth the child from sleeping: if it be too darke, it makes him desire the light, and causes him to be melancholike: if it be too hote, it will stifle him, & make him apt to catch cold, when he comes into the aire: if it be too cold, it brings him to a murre, or stopping in the head: and therefore it will be best to keep a meane in all of them: And especially you must have a care, that the Cradle, and bed, stand not neare the dore, chimney, or windowes, that the light do not draw the childs sight awrie, and so make him proove to be squint-ey'd: and therefore the fire, or the candle must be set right against his eyes: For if they were on either side, the glimpse will make the child turne and role his eye aside, to follow the light, and so the use and motion, which the Muscles would get therby, may make him either squint or goggle-ey'd.

Oftentimes the child cannot sleep after he is laid downe, and therefore he must be gently rock'd, to invite him thereto, and not hastily or too fast, for feare of making the milke flote in his stomacke; and his Nurse shall sing by him, because singing provokes sleepe, and keepes him from crying.

Till the childe be two yeere old, he may sleepe at all times whensoever he will, yea he may fall asleepe at his mothers teat as hee is sucking: and if you would observe the space of time for sleeping which the Ancients did, it must be thus: Till the childe be three or foure yeeres old, let him sleepe more than wake. But according to *Galen*, he ought heerein not to exceed mediocritie, otherwise it is dangerous: for long sleeping cooleth and moistneth the braine, and there retaines superfluities. And *Avicen* saith, that it doth be-numme and besot the childs senses, and makes him dull and lumpish.

When the Mother her selfe, or the Nurse, ought to give the child sucke, and how, and how much.

Chap. VI.

It is verie fit that either the Mother, or some other Nurse for her, do give the child sucke after he is borne: if it be the Mother her selfe, it must not be at the soonest, untill eight daies after her deliverie: Some also are of opinion, that the mother her selfe, should not give her child sucke in the month, by reason she hath been troubled and tir'd in her lying in: and because she is not as yet, well cleans'd and purified of her after-purgings, which commonly last a moneth, as *Hippocrates* saith: In which space she shall let little prettie whelpes sucke her breasts, to make her milke come the better, and that it goe not away.

Some women do make their keepers draw their breasts, and others draw them with glasses themselves: Besides, *Avicen* commands, that a woman should not give her child sucke, untill she be well recover'd. Now, you know that some are well sooner, and some later, and so there can be no time limited or prescribed: But above all it must be observed, (as the same Authour saith) that the Nurse do not give the child sucke, after she is risen, before she hath milked foorth some of her milke: And likewise, she shall not give him the breast, if by chance she hath over heated her selfe, either by some exercise, or else with going, till first she be come into a good temper, and well cool'd.

Now, in giving him sucke, she shall observe this order: She must sometimes spirt some of her milke, either upon the childs lips, or else into his mouth; and when he hath left the nipple, she must crush her breast a little, that he may draw and sucke with lesse labour, and she must be carefull, that he swallow not downe too much at a time, and that the milke come not out againe at the nose: Besides, she must sometimes take away the teat, and give it him againe, that he sucke not too much at once, and too greedily.

It is verie hard to set downe, the quantitie of milke that a child should take; But therein the nurse must have a respect to the age, complexion, temper, and to the desire which the child hath to sucke, increasing it, as the child groweth, or according as he is thirstie, either through some sicknesse, or when his teeth come foorth: for at those times he is more drie, then otherwise. Now to know how often the child should sucke in a day: *Paulus Aegineta* appoints, that it should be twise a day, or thrise at the most: which he meaneth for the first foure, or five daies, that he may be acquainted therewith by little and little, and also because there is then no great need. I have seen children that have not sucked in two or three daies, after they were borne; for they know not then, whether they are yet in their Mothers belly, or no: where they suck'd not at all; although that *Hippocrates* saith, that the child receives some nourishment by the mouth, while he is in his Mothers belly. It can neither be told nor limitted how often he ought to sucke in a day; because it is fit he should have the teat, as often as he crieth: yet let it be but a little at a time, because the stomacke at first is but weake. And if he wrangles but a little, it will be best to still him, either with rocking, or singing: And though he be not quieted, or stilled, a little crying can doe him no great harme, but rather may serve for some good use: For it makes him runne at Nose, shed teares, and spit: it purgeth his braine, yea, and stirreth up his naturall heat, and also dilates the passages of the breast. But if he cry too violently, and eagerly, it may do him much harm, and cause him to be bursten, or breake some vessell in his breast, or else bring the head-ach.

How the child must be made cleane, after he is awake and unswathed.

CHAP. VII.

After the Child hath well suck'd, and slept, the Nurse must shift him, and make him cleane: For which purpose the Nurse, or some other, must sit neere the fire, laying out her legges at length, having a soft pillow in her lap, the dores and windowes being close shut, and having something about her, that may keep the wind from the child. And when she is thus accommodated, she shall unswath and shift him drie. If he be verie foule, she may wash him with a little water and wine luke warme, with a spunge or linnen cloth.

The time of shifting him is commonly about seven a clocke in the morning, then againe at noone, and at seven a clocke at night: and it would not be amisse, to change him againe about midnight; which is not commonly done. But because there is no certaine howre, either of the childs sucking, or sleeping: therefore divers, after he hath slept a good while, do every time shift him: least he should foule and bepisse himselfe. And surely there be many children, that had need to be shifted, as soone as they have foul'd themselves: which I would counsaile you to doe, and not to let them lie in their filth.

When you change his bed, you shall rub all his bodie over, with an indifferent fine linnen cloth: and then his head must be rub'd, and made cleane: and when he is foure or five moneth old, his head may be cleans'd with a fine brush: and when he is growen bigger, let it be comb'd.

What cloths and coats the child must have,
and at what time.

CHAP. VIII.

As soone as the childe is somewhat growne, and that hee cannot well keepe his hands swathed in, and hid any longer, (which is commonly about the twentieth or thirtieth day, according as he is in strength) then must hee have little sleeves, that having his armes and hands at liberty, hee may use and stirre them: and then the Nurse shall begin to carry him abroad, so that it be faire weather, to sport and exercise him, not carrying him out into the raine, or into the hot sunne, nor when there is any rough wind.

And therfore he must be kept in the shade avoiding all ill ayres, as of sinkes and the like: And if he should chance to bee frighted with any thing, the Nurse shal endevor to take away the apprehension thereof, and harten him, without making him afraid. I have seen some children, that with a fright, have fallen into the *Epilepsye* or falling sicknes, the Physitions not being able to give any other reason thereof, but onely the feare he had taken.

If by chance he doth cry and weepe, then shall you endevour by all meanes to still him, and not let him cry, observing diligently what it is he cries for, and what may be the cause thereof: that as *Galen* saith, he may have that he desireth, or else be ridde of that which offends and troubleth him.

But the same Author saith, that children generally are stilled and quieted by three meanes: by giving them the breast, by rocking, and by singing to them: They may be also stilled by giving them something to holde in their hand, or by making them looke upon somwhat that pleaseth them, as also by carrying them abroad.

About the eighth, or ninth month, or at farthest when the child is a yeare old, he must have coates, and not be kept swathed any longer. And if it bee Sommer, he must be coated sooner because of the heate, which makes the body oftentimes, to be full of wheales and pimples. And some may have coats sooner, according as their strength will suffer it; of which an especiall care must be had. And chiefly the Nurse must let him have a hat, that may be easie and large enough, which may cover all the forepart of the head, without beeing curious (as they say commonly) to make him have a goodly high forhead.

At what age the child may take other sustenance beside Milke.

Chap. IX.

The childe must bee nourished with milk only, till his foreteeth be come forth both above, and beneath: as *Galen* writeth: for beeing nothing else yet but as it were milke it is very fit and probable that hee should bee nourished with no other foode: Besides the teeth are chiefly ordained by nature, onely to chaw: and therefore when he hath none, he ought not to be fed with any solide meat. But as soone as they are come forth it sheweth that Nature hath given him those instruments, to make use of them: and therefore hee may then take more solide meate, if you thinke he can digest it. For to give him any other nourishment, then milke or dish-meate, before hee have teeth, it might breede great store of crude humors, and winds, which oftentimes (as *Avicen* saith) doe cause the child to have bunches, or contusions, about his backe bone, and ribs. Neverthelesse, though his teeth bee come, yet must you not give him meat, that is too solide, or in too great quantitie: but at the beginning, you may give him sops of bread, or Panado, or Gruell: afterward he may suck the leg of a Chicken, the greatest part of the flesh being taken away, that he may the better pull, and gnaw it, and this is but once or twice a day, & that too, when he is almost ready to be weaned (as *Rhasis* saith.) And this also doth serve to whet and rub his gummes which about that time begin to itch. And when hee is fifteene moneths olde, or a little more, then may you give him the flesh of a Capon, or of Partridge minced and mingled with some broth, made either of Veale, Mutton, or Chicken, adding thereto some sops of bread. For the Ancient writers forbid, that wee should give them any store of meate, before they are two yeares old: because they are not able to chaw, and digest it, and also for that they have not so much neede of nourishment; And therefore you must stay till you have weaned him, before you feede him more plentifully.

When the child ought to be weaned.

CHAP. X.

It is a very hard thing to set downe a certaine time, when a child ought to be weaned; Notwithstanding if we wil beleeve *Paulus Aegineta*, and *Avicen*, he must be weaned, when he is two yeares old, and hath all his teeth come foorth. Now in some they come foorth sooner, and in others later: and to weane him before they are come foorth, might be an occasion, to make him have many diseases.

Wherefore to know certainely when a childe should be weaned, and that he should wholy feed upon other meat, it must first be observed, whether he take his meat well; and if hee be able to chaw it thoroughly: whether he be sickly or else strong and lusty.

Concerning the time and season of the yeare it must be when the wether is neither too hot, nor too cold: and therfore the fittest time will be the spring or in Autumn. But somtimes there is necessity to wean him at another time, yea & before two yeares, by reason that his nurse may chance to bee sickly, and that he being come to some knowledge will not sucke another. It may also happen that the child is to be weaned before he be two yeares old, for that the milke (although otherwise it bee good) doth curdle and grow sower in his stomacke, which requireth stronger meate.

Now to weane a childe well, let them observe this methode following: First the teat shall not be wholy taken from him, but hee shall sucke a little, and eate a little meate; and so continue for a few daies: then afterwards hee shall not sucke in the day time, though in the night, they may give him a little. Neverthelesse, it will be very fit in the morning, when he is awake and hath been shifted and dressed, to give him sucke a little, and then to let him stay two or three houres before hee take any thing, afterward to give him somwhat to dinner, as some pottage, or panade, with a little flesh minced, or cut very small, and then let him stay two houres without giving him any thing, at which time you may give him a little sucke, and lay him to sleepe: And when hee is wakened and hath beene made cleane, then the Nurse shall carry him abroad into the aire, if it be faire wether, and give him sucke, and then lay him to sleepe againe, without letting him eate any solide meate, or very little. At his dinner they shal give him to drinke a little boyled water: and this order shall bee kept a whole moneth, and when hee shall bee accustomed to eate soldie meate then the teate shall be quite taken from him.

It happens oftentimes that the child will not forsake the breasts, but still cryeth and is very eager after it, and then you must make him loath it, annointing the Nurses breast with Mustard, or else rubbing the top of the nipple with a little Aloes, and likewise make him ashamed of it.

Not all English mothers—native or colonial—wished to breast-feed their babies, and their reasons were as ingenuous as they were numerous. The least likely were the aristocracy, as one of their number accused in a pamphlet called The Countesse of Lincoln's Nurserie *(Oxford, 1622). Although American conditions may have been different for the aristocracy in the early years of settlement, the introduction of slavery and the formation of great plantations soon brought the southern gentry to a social position little different from that of their English ancestors of whom Elizabeth Lincoln spoke. The following passages are taken from the reprinted edition in* The Harleian Miscellany, *ed. William Oldys (London, 1809), vol. 4, pp. 27-33.*

Because it hath pleased God to bless me with many children, and so caused me to observe many things falling out to mothers, and to their children; I thought good to open my mind concerning a special matter belonging to all child-bearing women, seriously to consider of; and to manifest my mind the better, even to write of this matter, 'so far as God will please to direct me; in sum, the matter I mean, 'is the duty of nursing, due by mothers to their own children.'

In setting down whereof, I will, first, shew, that every woman ought to nurse her own child; and, secondly, I will endeavour to answer such objections, as are used to be cast out against this duty, to disgrace the same.

The first point is easily performed, for it is the express ordinance of God, that mothers should nurse their own children, and being his ordinance, they are bound to it in conscience. This should stop the mouths of all repliers; for God is most wise, and therefore must needs know what is fittest and best for us to do: and, to prevent all foolish fears, or shifts, we are given to understand, that he is also all-sufficient, and therefore infinitely able to bless his own ordinance, and to afford us means in ourselves (as continual experience confirmeth) toward the observance thereof.

If this (as it ought) be granted, then how venturous are those women that dare venture to do otherwise, and so to refuse, and, by refusing, to despise that order, which the most wise and all-mighty God hath appointed, and instead thereof to choose their own pleasures? O, what peace can there be to these women's consciences, unless, through the darkness of their understanding, they judge it no disobedience? . . .

Oh, consider, how comes our milk; is it not by the direct providence of God? Why provides he it, but for the child? The mothers then, that refuse to nurse their own children, do they not despise God's Providence? Do they not deny God's will? Do they not as it were say, 'I see, O God, by the means thou hast put into me, that thou wouldst have me nurse the child thou hast given me; but I will not do so much for thee.' Oh, impious and impudent unthankfulness; yea monstrous unnaturalness, both to their own natural fruit born so near their breasts, and fed in their own wombs, and yet may not be suffered to suck their own milk!

And this unthankfulness and unnaturalness is oftener the sin of the higher and the richer sort, than of the meaner and poorer; except some nice and proud idle dames, who will imitate their betters, till they make their poor husbands beggars. And this is one hurt which the better rank do by their ill example; egg and embolden the lower ones to follow them to their loss. Were it not better for us greater persons to keep God's ordinance, and to shew the meaner their duty in our good example? I am sure we have more helps to perform it, and have fewer probable reasons to allege against it, than women that live by hard labour, and painful toil. If such mothers as refuse this office of love, and of nature to their children, should hereafter be refused, despised, and neglected of those their children; were they not justly requited according to their own unkind dealing? I might say more in handling this first point of my promise; but I leave the larger and learneder discourse hereof unto men of art, and learning; only I speak of so much as I read, and know in my own experience; which if any of my sex and condition do receive good by, I am glad; if they scorn it, they shall have the reward of scorners. I write in modesty, and can reap no disgrace by their immodest folly.

And so I come to my last part of my promise; which is to answer objections made by divers against this duty of mothers to their children.

First, it is objected, that Rebecca had a nurse, and that therefore her mother did not give her suck of her own breasts, and so good women, in the first ages, did not hold them to this office of nursing their own children. To this I answer, that if her mother had milk, and health, and yet did put this duty from her to another, it was her fault, and so proved nothing against me. But it is manifest, that she that Rebecca called her nurse, was called so, either for that she most tended her while her mother suckled her; or for that she weaned her; or for that, during her nonage and childhood, she did minister to her continually such good things as delighted and nourished her up. For to any one of these the name of a nurse is fitly given; whence a good wife is called her husband's nurse; and that Rebecca's nurse was only such a one, appeareth, because afterwards she is not named a nurse, but a maid, saying: 'Then Rebecca rose, and her maids;' now maids give not suck out of their breasts, never any virgin or honest maid gave suck, but that blessed one from an extraordinary and blessed power.

Secondly, it is objected that it is troublesome; that it is noisome to one's clothes; that it makes one look old, &c. All such reasons are uncomely and unchristian to be objected, and therefore unworthy to be answered; they argue unmotherly affection, idleness, desire to have liberty to gad from home, pride, foolish fineness, lust, wantonness, and the like evils. Ask Sarah, Hannah, the blessed Virgin, and any modest loving mother, what trouble they accounted it to give their little ones suck? Behold most nursing mothers, and they be as clean and sweet in their clothes, and carry their age, and hold their beauty, as well as those that suckle not, and most likely are they so to do; because, keeping God's ordinance, they are sure of God's blessing; and it hath been observed in some women, that they grew more beautiful, and better favoured, by very nursing their own children.

But there are some women that object fear, saying that they are so weak, and so tender, that they are afraid to venture to give their children suck, lest they endanger their health thereby. Of these, I demand, 'Why then they did venture to marry, and so to bear children?' And if they say they could not choose, and that they thought not that marriage would impair their health: I answer, that for the same reasons they should set themselves to nurse their own children, because they should not choose, but to do what God would have them to do; and they should believe that this work will be for their health also, seeing it is ordinary with the Lord to give good stomach, health, and strength to almost all mothers that take this pains with their children.

One answer more to all the objections, that use to be made against giving children suck, is this, that now the hardness, to effect this matter, is much removed by a late example of a tender young lady; and you may all be encouraged to follow after, in that wherein she hath gone before you, and so made the way more easy, and more hopeful, by that which she findeth possible and comfortable by God's blessing, and no offence to her lord and herself; she might have had as many doubts, and lets, as any of you, but she was willing to try how God would enable her, and he hath given her good success, as I hope he will do to others that are willing to trust in God for his help.

Now if any reading these few lines return against me, "that it may be I myself have given my own children suck, and therefore am bolder and more busy to meddle in urging this point, to the end to insult over, and to make them to be blamed that have not done it." I answer, that whether I have, or have not, performed this my bounden duty; I will not deny to tell my own practice. I know and acknowledge that I should have done it, and having not done it, it was not for want of will in myself, but partly I was over-ruled by another's authority, and partly deceived by some ill counsel, and partly I had not so well considered of my duty in this motherly office, as since I did, when it was too late for me to put it in execution. Whereof being pricked in heart for my undutifulness, this way, I study to redeem my peace, first, by repentance towards God, humbly and often craving his pardon for this my offence; secondly, by studying how to shew double love to my children, to make them amends for neglect of this part of love to them, when they should have hung on my breasts, and have been nourished in my own bosom; thirdly, by doing my endeavour to prevent many Christian mothers from sinning, in the same kind, against our most loving and gracious God . . .

Do you submit yourselves to the pain and trouble of this ordinance of God? Trust not other women, whom wages hires to do it, better than yourselves, whom God and nature tie to do it. I have found, by grievous experience, such dissembling in nurses, pretending sufficiency of milk, when indeed they had too much scarcity; pretending willingness, towardness, wakefulness, when indeed they have been most wilful, most forward, and most slothful; as I fear the death of one or two of my little babes came by the default of their nurses. Of all those which I had for eighteen children, I had but two which were thoroughly willing and careful: divers have had their children miscarry in the nurses' hands, and are such mothers (if it were by the nurses' carelessness) guiltless? I know not how they should, since they will shut them out of the arms of nature, and leave them to the will of a stranger; yea, to one that will seem to estrange herself from her own child, to give suck to the nurse-child. This she may feign to do upon a covetous composition, but she frets at it in her mind, if she has any natural affection.

Therefore be no longer at the trouble, and at the care, to hire others to do your own work; be not so unnatural as to thrust away your own children; be not so hardy as to venture a tender babe to a less tender heart; be not accessary to that disorder of causing a poorer woman to banish her own infant, for the entertaining of a richer woman's child, as it were, bidding her unlove her own to love yours. We have followed Eve in transgression, let us follow her in obedience. When God laid the sorrows of conception, of breeding, of bringing forth, and of bringing up her children upon her, and so upon us in her loins; did she reply any word against it? Not a word: so I pray you all my own daughters, and others that are still childbearing, reply not against the duty of suckling them, when God hath sent you them.

Indeed, I see some, if the weather be wet, or cold; if the weather be foul, if the church be far off, I see they are so coy, so nice, so lukewarm, they will not take pains for their own souls. Alas! No marvel if these will not be at trouble and pain to nourish their children's bodies; but fear God, be diligent to serve him; approve all his ordinances, seek to please him; account it no trouble or pain to do anything that hath the promise of his blessing; and then you will, no doubt, do this good, laudable, natural, loving duty, to your children . . .

Birth is an intimate affair and seldom does notice of it come into the public record. The following items are among the few for colonial Virginia. The first two come from The Calendar of Virginia State Papers 1652-1781, *ed. W.P. Palmer (Richmond, 1875), vol. 1, pp.*

9, 143. The third, showing an unusual form of freedom contract for a Negro slave woman, is the will of John Guthrie dated 17 October 1761. It is taken from Judicial Cases Concerning American Slavery and the Negro, ed. Helen T. Catterall (Washington, 1926), vol. 1, pp. 103-104.

To the Right Honoble Sir William Berkeley, Let. Governor, Capt. Genl. of Virginia, and to the Honble Councell of State.

John Edwards. humbly showeth,

That in October last yr Petitioner in zeal to God's Glory and true obedience to his Majties lawes, did exhibit twoe prsentmts to the Worshipll the Court of Lower Norfolke: against John Biggs of the same County, the which, wth their circumstances and aggravacons did purport matters and things tending to the high dishonor of Almighty God, and distructive to the peasse and wellfare of his Majties good subjects, which Worshipll Court made noe finalle result of; therefore yr petitioner appealed to his Honoble Court, that whereas the said John Biggs, contrary to the ordinances of the Church of England, established in this Collony, refuseth to come to church, and alsoe refuseth to christen his children, which is alsoe contrary to severall Acts of Parliamt, and an Act of Assembly, in that case, made and provided. And yr petitioner humbly prays yor Worsll Judgmts herein, and alsoe to grant yor Petitioner the benefitt of the Acts wth his charges.

And as in duty bound shall ever pray, &.

Know all all men, whom this may concern:

That whereas, John Bigges was Ordered by our County Court, held in Apprill, to bring his children to the Holy Ordinance of Baptism, by the 12th of May next ensuing: Hee, thee said John, did neither bring nor send them to be baptized by me, the present minister of Elizabeth River parish, by the time appointed.

As witness, my hand this 12th of June, 1675.
WILLIAM HARNE.

An Act to prevent the destroying & murthering of Bastard Children—

Whereas several Lewd women that have been delivered of Bastard Children, to avoid their shame and escape punishment, do secretly bury or conceal the death of their children, and after, if the child be found dead, the said Women do alledge, that the said Child was born dead; whereas it falleth out sometimes (although hardly it is to be proved) that the sd: child or children were murthered by the said Women, their Lewd Mothers or by their assent or procurement. For preventing therefore this great mischeif, Be it Enacted by the Lieutenant Governor, Council and Burgesses of this present General Assembly, and it is hereby Enacted by the Authority of the same, That if any woman after one moneth next ensuing the end of this present Session of Assembly, be delivered of any issue of her body, male or female, which being born alive, should by Law, be a bastard, and that she endevour privately, either by drowning, or secret burying thereof, or any other way, either by herself, or the procuring of others, to conceal the death thereof, as that it may not come to light, whether it were born alive or not, but be concealed; in every such case, the mother so offending, shal suffer Death, as in case of murther; Except such mother can make proof by one witness, at the least, that the child (whose death was by her so intended to be concealed) was born dead.

pass'd in Council Novemb ye 8th 1710

November 2d Read the first time
November 6th Read the Second time

My will is that my son Richard should have his choyes of my 2 whences [wenches] Geany or Dice [Negro slaves] and if he chuses upon Jeany and she should bring ever so many children she shall nurce them till they are fourteen months old an then shall return them to James Guthrie or his ears [heirs], but if he chuses upon Dice he shall have her and her ears . . [8] my will is that all Jeaneys children that is now living (viz.) I give unto James Guthrie and his ears forever, Harry, Daffenny, Frank and Samson, my will is if Richard Guthrie makes choyes of Jeany he shall have no other part of estate, my will is that Richard Guthrie should have Dice and London and her increase and to his ears forever, my will is that Jeany and all her increase shall be James Guthries and his ears forever moreover my will is that if Jeany brings ten live children that she shall be at her one [own] liberty from him or his eares only living with James Guthrie or his ears her lifetime.

The best source for child-bearing practices is the uninhibited diary and Landon Carter's is one of the best. Born in 1710 to Robert "King" Carter of Corotoman plantation, Virginia, one of the wealthiest men in America, Landon became one of the typical Virginia planters of his day. Educated in England and married at 22 when he inherited eight plantations upon his father's death, he sired seven children who survived to adulthood, outlived three wives, and served faithfully as a county and colonial official. He died in 1778, leaving an estate of 50,000 acres and 500 slaves to the children whose behavior tormented him all their days. The following selections are taken from The Diary of Colonel Landon Carter of Sabine Hall, 1752-1778, *ed. Jack P. Greene (Charlottesville, 1965), 2 vols.*

1766: 7 July. A prodigeous rain yesterday about 2 and to near 4. We had though Sunday as a work of great necessity as our bread depended on it for we could buy no corn any where. . . .

I was just riding out to see the destruction but was called back by my son to his wife then taken in labour the 3d time without a midwife so punctual are women or rather obstinate to their false accounts. I found every body about her in a great fright and she almost in dispair. The child was dead and the womb was fallen down and what not. I found her pulse good and even though as all women in such cases are and I believe should be; I knew that this could be no prolapses of the womb till after a delivery but from the accounts concluded it might be the Vagina swelled and inflamed. I therefore ordered it to be gently pressed up with Marsh Mallow decoction and milk. At last this proved only the protuberance of the waters through the thickness of the membrane. Those broke and a large dead child much squeezed and indeed putrified was delivered. An intire placenta but no lochial discharge. Another prodigeous alarm. I could not but say that I did not like it, but reasoned from the dead state of the fetus the possibility of such a circumstance though I never read of it in any Author; but as I know all authors do say if the woman is well and free from fevers or violent pain the colour nor quantity of the lochia is not to be regarded, and as this is Mrs. Carter's real state I hope no danger. I ordered her in some cordial gruel (which I had all along directed her) about 20 grains Ipecacuana which brought on a breathing moisture and then a Lochial discharge came on. This is a disagreeable state for me to be in where I see the ingratitude of those for whom I give myself such concern; but they will never be provided against accident with mid wives and Doctors and are human creatures. Dr. Mortimer came here and sees as yet nothing amiss. I am glad he is, it is a releif to me; for I do believe ten thousand anticipations are every moment broached without the least foundation; it is the effect of tenderness; but great weakness.

1770: 27 March.   This day we intended to have Bob Carter's little child baptized. By the whim of our Minister all Children must be christened in Church. I wrote to him yesterday that we should be there unless it was bad weather and asked if he could not, should it prove bad weather, perform that service at home as Mr. John Wormeley who is to be a Godfather was here and impatient to get down. His answer acknowledges he had done so for others but as he had gained nothing but censure in such compliances, imagining I hinted at them, he was determined in preserving in his resolution in baptizing no Children out of the Church. I gave no cause for this and am only convinced it is a full explanation. That this Gentleman rather makes a use of all instances relative to me [to] confirm his oddities in these things imagining that as others see he does them to me to whom they must reasonably conclude he lies under some obligation for the long time he lived here at free cost they will not solicit him to break through his obligations to others. But upon the whole I must say his pleading his oath to conform to the Canons not settled with the least view to the situation of [torn] Countries where the professors [of] Christianity must probably live at [Gr]eat distance from the Churches I [say th]is conformity is rather an excuse [torn] off for him to avoid to trouble [torn] the same conformity must [torn] man not to marry people but in churches. However as he is paid a fee there both for the license and even for marrying upon being asked in church he prefers going to houses where the fee expected is greater than allowed for a license and as to the asking fee by marrying them always at home he gets the money without the trouble of going abroad. Besides if they will go to the Canon that I believe directs the Baptism to be performed during divine service which by the by is never done and much in the mode of gratifying the aversion to trouble for it is easier after divine service is over to go to the font than to be walking backwards and forwards during divine service which I fancy my friend is not fond of for he goes as seldom to the Alta[r] in the church service as any Min[is]ter as I have ever been acquain[ted] with. However I impeach his [torn] fault. He has many good qu[alities] and I wish he had not this [torn].

14 October. Mrs. Carter [his daughter-in-law] taken ill yesterday and was to be seen so before, though she would not own it. And the poor little baby Fanny is every time to share her Mama's disorder by sucking her, and this because she should not breed too fast. Poor children! Are you to be sacrificed for a parent's pleasure?

I have been a Parent and I thought it murder and therefore hired nurses or put them out.

Little Fanny Carter ever since fryday last has had from 4 to near 8 a daily ague, the most violent by account that a grown person generally has, and then a fever.

They would follow no advice of mine. Dr. Mortimer was sent for; saw her in one of these agues, ordered her a vomit, which I had done before; he did not stay to see it work, but expressly forbid the bark to be used pretending the fits would return, and yet directed nothing to keep them off, though he was as certain they would keep on whether she took bark or not; and these weak or rather Obstinate Parents were against using the bark to this poor babe when every fit was a mere death. However I was at last [indulged] in the use of 3 doses of 6 grains each with a little Rhubarb yesterday. The fit kept its period, but my wench told me not so violent nor so long; and as the fever went off in a plentifull sweat I continued the doses encreased to 10 grains; but now the child will only suck its mother's milk poisoned with her very bilious habit; and madam pretends she will spit spoon victuals out and will not give her any even as a medicine. In short, I never knew such a vile, obstinate woman, even beyond a human creature, whilst her husband tallys in with her stupidity. And I suppose by and by if the child dies the creature will be then whindling for what she herself has done.

1771: 26 August. My son's Wife miscarried last night. She is a strange woman. I suspected her being with child some months ago, and advized her to be carefull in many things, particularly to get timely blooded, as she always knew how fatal the want of [s]uch a thoughtfulness had been [torn] a laughing matter, both in her husband and herself; till on Saturday whilst Colo. Corbin, his son, and daughter was here she was taken with very suspicious complaints, concea[led] from everybody, for she went about as Usual; and after the Company was gone she would only be blooded in the morning. Yesterday she was blooded, and stayed from bre[ak]fast to keep herself still, the only piece of prudence she has been guilty of. And in order to keep her to it her husband stayed at home all day yesterday. But when I came home last night I found Mortimer was sent for: however after much uneasiness she miscarried about 11. And upon inquiry I find this still Lady came down yesterday to dinner, eat heartily of Mutton Chops, fish etc., and cherry tart with milk in it: So that to all appearance there must have been some intention to forward the abortio[n]. Strange woman indeed; it is not [torn].

1772: 18 August. It is curious to hear so often as we do that because clouds can't be seen through at any good distance People at least 5 miles off will be knowing better how it has rained at another man's house than he does himself who from being long parched up with drowth must necessarily be intent on looking at the prodigeous blessing of rain in such a wofull state; and of course more disposed to magnifie every drop that falls than be the least inclined to lessen it. Thus my son at Capt. Beale's all day yesterday full 5 miles off, because he had rode by some puddles in a baked dry road should violent suspect me of Untruth when I told him at the house and further on from the river the rain was in some plenty but towards the river where all my corn and tobacco crop lay it was but moderate, and whilst the cloud was falling here myself and two more gentlemen within doors took notice that the sky was clear all below my hill; and this bread almost the alteration of my telling a lie; such is his constant genius for contradiction especially to his father. Certainly the most unnatural and most graceless of all behaviour. His wife truely who must only have confined herself to her chamber in her heavy state, and could only see the rain going from the river, had the decency to join with him; to explain from whence this prodigeous vein of contradiction must have at first originated; but I have long known this; and she will probably find that I do know it, in spight of all her Princesslike art; for I do beleive women have nothing in the general in view, but the breeding contests at home. It began with poor Eve and ever since then has been so much of the devil in woman.

1774: 1 October. Mrs. Carter very well yesterd[ay], though very big with child, must needs go to visit Mrs. Lomax, lately laid in, and came home very well and so continued untill I went to bed at 8 o'clock. Her husband like a fool sure of his wife's Punctuality in reackoning, though I often told him the woman must not be without a midwife, Pretended to be sure she would not want one before November. And away goes he on his diversions Up to Fredricksburgh.

This morning no madam to breakfast. I desired to know what was the matter, could get no answer, although I sent her son up to ask in my name; but nothing was the word. At last just as breakfast was over everybody was on the run for somebody, nobody can tell who; the woman in labour and now it comes out; she had not felt her child these 2 months; a thing she had never spoak of to one soul. But now it seems she says she told me she was not with child, and that was intended to discover the Child was dead within her, just as if a woman with a dead child in her, could be thought much more said not to be with child; and this insisted on even by Miss Lucy.

Half after 9 a dead child born, but no afterbirth can be got away, for she has not even a pain. I sent for Jones. Perhaps Madam will make my words good, She has always been fond of such a hurry; and it is Possible that has fooled her out of her life. As nobody could be instantly got to this distressed but really undeserving woman, after I had ordered her to be put to bed, and had given about 2 hours time to nature to do her own office of expulsion of the Placenta if it could, I ventured to assist her with an active draught or two, which brought on a Proper pain and in about 10 minutes she was well cleared as I am told of everything that should come away.

Her Son Landon went to fetch Mrs. Falkes from Mrs. Jones' where she was attending her lying in; and, though my Chariot went for her, she did not come till about half an hour after she was cleared. I directed her to make her inquiries, and if all was as things should be, to let her be kept quiet for a good Sleep. This I understood she was got into, and then I laid down to recover myself from the bad Colic effects of this ill contrived alarm, and in the time Dr. Jones came, which could not be before 12; about 1, I awaked, and the Dr. came down and went away with Mrs. Falks to his Lady, Pronouncing all things well. I could not get him to stay even to dinner; therefore he has done nothing, should any reputation arise from a recovery of this ill contrived, obstinate woman.

2 October. Hear nothing from Mrs. Carter as yet, only all were quiet in her room at daybreak and I was [to]ld all things were as they should [be] in quantity, Colons and smell Particularly enquired into; because this is an extraordinary Case: A child quite rotten and fetid brought and without pain, and, though the Placenta forced away, no taint at all in it nor no Lochial discharge discolored or fetid. It seems there was water enough discharged both before and after the birth to have drowned any fetus, had no fright have happened August 2, which it seems, as I am told, so told, did happen on a visit she made her brother Tho. Beale then.

It is her own fault, a woman that hardly moves when not with child, always is Jolting in a Chariot when with Child. This is the 3d destroyed this way.

By most men's standards Landon Carter should have been a happy man. He was not. For despite his great wealth, his social and political influence, and his intellectual independence, he was plagued most of his life by a brood of children and grandchildren whose unbridled behavior threatened to bury the family name in ignominy. The following excerpts from his Diary *edited by Jack P. Greene (Charlottesville, 1965) chronicle his growing unhappiness.*

1757: 24 October. This day near Sunset Landon Carter [Junior] came home. I with great mildness asked him if he did not think that as he was to go up to Bull Hall tomorrow he ought to have staid at home to have taken my directions with regard to my affairs and if he did not think this Sauntering about from house to house only to inflame himself the more by visiting a woman that he knew I would never Consent to his marrying would not ruin him and contrary to his duty. He answered very calmly No. Then Sir be assured that although you will shortly be of age if you do not henceforward leave her you must leave me. He answer, then Sir I will leave you, on which I bid him be gone out of my house. He took up his hat and sayd so he would as soon as he could get his horse and went off immediately without shewing the least Concern, no not even to turn round. This I write down the moment it passed that I might not through want of memory omit so Singular an act of great filial disobedience in a Child that I have thought once my greatest happyness but as a just Father kept it concealed.

13 December. It is necessary that man should be acquainted with affliction and 'tis certainly nothing short of it to be confined a whole year in tending one's sick Children. Mine are now never well. Indeed I may believe there are many reasons for it besides the Constitution of the air which has been very bad. I have none but negroes to tend my children nor can I get anyone and they use their own children to such loads of Gross food that they are not Judges when a child not so used to be exposed to different weathers and not so inured to exercise Comes to eat. They let them press their appetites as their own children did and thus they are constantly sick. Judy Carter, who has been as well for many weeks as ever child was, by being suffered after her dinner to some of her sister's barley broth yesterday took in such a load as could not be contained in her stomach and this day she was seized with a natural vomiting. I found nothing but food coming up and therefore ordered a small dose of Ipecacuana to help to clear the over burthened Stomach. The medi[ci]n I gave produced a while good effects by bringing off a good deal of filth and Bile but it had too powerfull an effect on her weak stomach for she vomited 6 times yellow bile, and whether an ague intevened I don't know but she lost her pulse for two hours and quite dead coldness and hardly alive with nervous Catchings in her hands and Jaws so that I fancyed her death near. However I gave her Pulvis Cantian 5 grains, Salt tartar 5 grains, Pulvis Castor 2 grains in a weak Julep of Rum, water and

mint and in about 2-1/2 hours her pulse beat and after a good sleep Nature seemed to recover and a Small fever ensued which wore away by night gradually and the Child mended, grew cheerfull and had an appetite to eat which I sparingly indulged but she lost all her bloom off her face this morning.

II. GROWTH

Even the rich can fall into the generation gap. How did Landon Carter's children and grandchildren act toward him? What economic as well as personal reasons might account for their behavior? What was the aristocratic ideal of social relations? What authority or power did parents have to enforce it? How and by whom were gentry children educated? What is education? What were the educational duties—formal and informal—of the plantation tutor? of the parents? Were boys and girls educated differently? What education did slaves and servants receive? Was the tutor's lot a happy one? What was his social position in the family? Did this create any problems of discipline?

1766: 27 June. We had this day a domestic gust. My daughters, Lucy and Judy, mentioned a piece of impudent behaviour of little Landon to his mother; telling her when she said she would whip him, that he did not care if she did. His father heard this unmoved. The child denied it. I bid him come and tell me what he did say for I could not bear a child should be sawsy to his Mother. He would not come and I got up and took him by the arm. He would not speak. I then shook him but his outrageous father says I struck him. At Breakfast the Young Gent. would not come in though twice called by his father and once Sent for by him and twice by me. I then got up, and gave him one cut over the left arm with the lash of my whip and the other over the banister by him. Madame then rose like a bedlamite that her child should be struck with a whip and up came her Knight Errant to his father with some heavy God damning's, but he prudently did not touch me. Otherwise my whip handle should have settled him if I could. Madam pretended to rave like a Madwoman. I shewed the child's arm was but commonly red with the stroke; but all would not do. Go she would and go she may. I see in her all the ill treatment my son gives and has given me ever since his marriage. Indeed I always saw this in her a girl a Violent, Sulkey, Proud, imperious Dutch so One fit to be the Queen of a Prince as the old—always complimented her. As this child is thus encouraged to insult me, I have been at great expence hitherto in maintaining him but I will be at no more. And so I shall give notice.

1771: 16 June. I was sorry to see what I did yesterday, and therefore sorry from the sinc[e]rity of my heart to say that if wanted or could be gratifyed in knowing that my son would have a full measure meted to him of all the insults which he has frequently though imprudently offered me, and often confessedly for his diversion; for his son not void of sence but void of all filial decency will from a temper too visible in the appearance of it to be denied from whence he inherits it, in a very little time become the most outrageous of all children that ever lived. In short, his indulgence of that temper is so constant and extravagant that I doubt not but in a little time he will turn everybody out of doors if he can. It is now above ten days since he began to unrein it, and except when he wants to be obliged in anything that he cannot get, he never behaves now with common decency to anyone Soul, either to me, his Father, his mother, his Aunts, his sister, his brother, nay even to the smallest babies when out of temper, and that is now almost always.

No rain but heavy in clouds is the morning as for some time past.

I made it my business out of duty to talk to this Grandson and namesake, and set before him the unhappiness he must throw everybody into as well as himself, for he must be dispised by all his relations. At first he endeavoured to avoid me, and went away. I bid him come back; he pretended to be affraid that I wanted to scold at him. I told him no, it was my concern that made me earnest to advise him to imploy his good sence which god had blessed him with, and not to sacrifice that to a temper which must in the end make him miserable. At last he seemed to listen, and indeed shed tears at what I said. I hope in God then he will learn to behave better.

1772: 14 January. Some people cheat the world by their tears. They first get into a great passion, and then Pass off their crying [as] a tenderness in their disposition. This day I saw mother and daughter smearing the butter they had helped themselves to over their plates: I laught and took notice how exactly one imitated the other. At which the old crying Pattern first got to bouncing at me; I bid her not get into a Passion for she knew I never minded that. At which she burst out into an alarming flood of tears, and cryed it away with abundance of impudent charge against my partiality to Lucy who by the by I am always every day finding fault with for her thoughtless behaviour. I cautioned her to keep to the truth and not to let her passions carry her out of the bounds of it; for she knew I was constantly reprehending Lucy for many things. In short I too constantly see the obstinacy of this Lady in her eldest son and daughter; The first she entirely has ruined by storming at me whenever I would have corrected him a child; and the other has already got to be as sawsy a Minx as ever sat at my table. She can't eat brown bread, nor bread without toasting; She cannot drink Coffee, etc. So that at about 13 years she is a compleat Lady Townley.

25 June. It seems that my respectful Son's Son is going soon to the College; and I dare pronounce for what, to make him the most outrageous scoundrel that ever appeared in human Shape. I this day saw an instance of filial behaviour to his mother that would have shocked me, had I not most sensibly known that this woman together with his father has contributed to ruin one of the most orderly boys of his time, by bellowing out to take him from under a very Just correction I was many years ago going to give him, for even an insult to that very woman.

This youth going to the College was in want of some necessaries such as handkerchiefs which his parents had not. I thought of some in my chest and offered if they would do to give them for his use. It seems he had before seen them and had wished I would give them to him, which I did not know of. But upon seeing them making up he dashed them down and swore he would not have them, and on being asked what had intitled him to better, as they had them not, Then he immediately asked his mother what had intitled her to better, and upon her replying that then she was only upon a level with him, to which with warmth he asked what had intitled her to be any more than upon a level. If from this Speciman the blade don't make good my Prophecy of his revenging the ill usage I have ever received from his Parent I will venture to be hanged.

3 October. The Squire raves and insults when at home and beds 3/4 past 7. He fears no Lord but the Lord of hosts; would to God he does not forget to fear him soon, for to be sure when Principles of order and society decline, other duties must, and I am much mistaken if duty to Parents is not within the scripture rule. How can you love God whom you have not seen, and dispise Parents who you have seen. I am tortured with this species of filial disrespect. How does he condemn the terribility of a certain relation that shocks his father, who seems to boast of shocking his own Parent Out of mere wantonness charged with Corotoman and Landon down for not blacking over my lead pencil O's. It must have been before or as soon as Webb came here and that was in about 3 years after my first wife died in 1740. So that this fact asserted must have been 33 or 34 years ago. A fine memory in a child to arraign an old father about. Some can fancy first and then swear to it as a truth.

1774: 12 February. My son came from Corotoman yesterday; but he never went to see my estate. He has truely got the name of Wild Bob; for there is not one kind of business he cares for but that of gaming and running about. In short, he is every man's man but his own and his father's, never at home hardly, and when at home, unless upon some trifling imployment, he sleeps all day; for he never reads. This has gaming produced and this the example that he sets his son; both fine Ginius murdered. Perhaps with what they have got they may Pass with the rest of mankind, some of whom are but Idiots.

12 August. If ever man can be truely said to be Cursed with a Child it must be I; and with my eldest son too, for whom I have ever been doing the most tender of kindnesses; but ingratitude with him is a virtue especially to his Parent. I foresaw that this would be the case when he was making his connections. An old froe knew my tenderness to a child and therefore run all hazards. Like a fool, although he made them intirely against his avowed and Solem declarations to me, and of course against my will, in order, if possible, to win this brute over to me when he had not one farthing to depend upon, I gave him an estate that anyone but mere dissipation could with the most common care could make £300 a year out of and this with no kind of Expence to him or his family, but a bare cloathing and that not to one of his Children, for him I maintained untill he was taught

to rebel against me; and so they are one after another, excepting Poor George, who I must Provide for, as I am sure will not be worth a shilling to leave him; because if he is not gaming away all and more than he makes, he is at Sleep on the Chairs or up in his bedchamber; and at all times if any Company come to the house he endeavours to get them to Cards so that I hardly have the Pleasure of a word's conversation of any one of them; for they play to bedtime and that to very late hours. In short, if ever this brute did one complasant thing to his father I will agree that I have not common sense. Everybody must see. Even at dinner he picks out all titbits, then asks everybody to have them and at last asks his father. Such a creature I would leave to the punishment of his God; but I fear I shall fall into some revenge for all this abominable ill treatment; as to be sure it is past all bearing. I have tried every way to be better treated, but cannot even Purchase it of him; many are the Pounds that I have paid out of my Pocket for him; but nothing will do. It was not long agoe besides the money I ordered him in town he converted some tobacco of mine to cash for his own use.

6 October. As on tuesday last I saw a certain Young Gentleman reading the fowl copy of my Codicil whilst it was lying on this table. Perhaps he may some day have the Curiosity to read this book; therefore I choose to give him a few sentiment relative to himself. I have often advised him to read and that no house that he can go to can be proper at this time of his life where the Company are disposed to a mere dissipation to Pass away life, let it be where it will; for there he will fall into gaming, at least the art of playing, and in that I do maintain lies the root of all Vice whatever.

At this particular time, when his mother is confined from Circumstances to her room, his father abroad, and the women naturally tired with her constant [illegible], one would have thought a grateful son not overdone with Pleasure might have staid at home or have seen her every 6 or 8 hours by way of Comfort to her in confinements. Or if a grandson had the grace to know his grandfather from whom his all must come he would when that Grandfather in extreme age and great infermity was alone attended with vast Pain have now and then endeavoured to have entertained him by his Company. But instead of all this he has been now 2 nights and near two days from home; but says a female connexion he was with his tother Grandfather. Yes he was so, learning the art of whist and betting in a [illegible], a fine improvement for one on whom a Country ought to look for Prudent advice and assistance.

I wonder the more that this has been done immediately after reading my Codicil as before; because had he minded that, it was Shewing that Obedience to Parents is much a duty to God and nature that from the first offence of that sort in the world, the fall of man, he might see that no redemption of the punishment inflicted was attempted, but only to put contrition in a way to avoid the dreadful effects of it, by a steady attention to work out man's future salvation only obtained to fallen man by Jesus christ. Death being an essential part of the Punishment, it could not be mitigated but as its eternal effects. Therefore in vain do they fancy who say we are to forgive as we expect to be forgiven, as if that forgiveness was of any thing but of real injuries, for the punishments of offences against nature seem according to my divinity not so much a personal injury as a disobedience that must overturn nature if not Prevented. For though the Prodigal eat the fatted calf of forgiveness we read the obedient Child was ever with his father and all that he had was his. If this is the certain reward of Natural obedience; to be sure the forgiveness of disobedience was only a motive to encourage a resistance and not to blot out the offence against nature once committed. By this reasoning that which is written may be truely reconciled and no harshness committed on the Petition before mankind or its intention; for man has injuries enough to be forgiven and to forgive; but offences against nature it is to be hoped he cannot turn.

24 December. I sent for my horse and desired the person who rode him never to come to S[abine] Hall any more whilst I lived; and so I told his temporizing Parent who pretends to find out that young fellow can't be restrained. So that Solomon was a damned fool when he said spare the rod and spoil the child; for if a young fellow has not sense enough to be restrained, why should a child be expected to have more? Master Solomon must also have been barbarous.

But this is all stuff; this father knows even this youth can be restrained and even by him if he would, but he knows it fluxes me to see so much dissipation and rather than not injoy his hopes of my quietus he is willing to Sacrifice his son. It is not his tenderness as a father or a master that he does thus; no, it is because he is fond of torturing his father. I never had a greater fondness than for this father and son, and both are going the same way. God send that those who wait for my estate may wait long enough, for I would willingly save a Soul or two alive before I die.

25 December. It seems the letter I wrote desiring my Grandson not to come to S[abine] Hall whilst I lived was read with great concern by him and at last by Mr. Ball. The first said Lord have mercy upon him; and the 2d said fye upon it Sir, come no more out a hunting, as it seems to be so disagreeable. The Youth came home, and when I was alone came to me. I asked him if he had not seen the letter I sent by Nassau. He said yes. I asked him why he came here any more; tears and contrition then flowed and upon a resolution to amend I welcomed him once more and shook hands. God almighty send he may be thoughtfull and then he will do well; that alone can save him.

I told him he was welcome to ride the horse as usual Provided he resolved to be advised, but not otherwise. I wanted nothing but to be happy in a good Prospect of his own happiness. He had Capacity and Constitution, and it would be a pitty that both should die away through dissipation; and as to an estate that might be a good one; but then he must make it one by deserving it.

I bid him to know, that I never would give over striving to save him whilst under my roof, as it was both from nature and Social tie a duty encumbent on me; and if he would not be advised, he must leave S[abine] Hall, where I wished him with all my soul to live long and happy. He said he would alter and hoped I would believe him.

1775: 11 September. Yesterday I walked up to my daughter Judith in the church, though I at the door, to ask her how she did and she hardly took notice of me. At Night, I received a letter from her which from one of less sense might be overlooked, but from her it carried all the Airs of a Species of revenge because I would not take her offending husband into favour. My son who cannot get help Piping to his wife's affections, endeavoured much to get this unaccountable man restored, Pretending more contrition in him than I dare say he will ever shew on the occasion and Robin would have had a mild tender answer written. But I put her in mind of her behaviour and in answer said that, although it would be condescending to her dutifull [behavior] and set a bad example to disobedient Children, Yet she and her husband might come where they pleased and stay as long as [they] would at S[abine] Hall, only declaring I would accommodate myself to such a trial if possible. Thus my God have I suffered myself to destroy thy divine order in governing this world; but thy religion is not only full of forgiveness but of the Social Virtue of forgetting injuries, though against the texture with which thou has made man and all for that grand and adorable end of a truely Social Virtue. We are thy imperfect beings in points of right and wrong; but I beseech thee let this not be imputed to me as a crime. I have laboured and can only justify myself by the means of thy word possibly imperfectly conceived by me. And, if it is not too offensive to thy Justice in Mercy, save us all.

1776: 22 July. However incredible this relation may be of any animated part of the creation except the brutes, I hereby call God to witness the truth of it. Colo. Robert Wormeley Carter, who surely has been somehow changed since born of his mother, though this day at dinner, though at my own table and with my own victuals, seeing me take a little vinegar out of the cucumber plate called out to his daughter to put some more vinegar and pepper in, for his father had taken it all out as he always does. I vow to God I had not more than half a teaspoonful to acidulate some oyster broth. I have dreaded what this filial disobedience will get to. I must be provided with pistols; for I am certain no resolution of mine can otherwise guard against the consequence. Lord, is not the 5th command, honor thy father and mother, and is this honor, gracious God?

1777: 19 May. This Page I have particularly devoted to set down the instances in which Colo. Robert Carter, my son, as he is said to be, so certainly differs from me in sentiment; and glories in recrimination as if it was comfortable to go to hell in company. But he should remember if I am to be accused in differing with any person out of the Spirit of contradiction it cannot be any charge against me of doing it with my father so that I am quite clear of the 5th Command in this accusation. But that command truely was only given to Children and not to persons above 40 years of age.

8 August. Jesse came down again for old Mrs. Hamilton and brought me a letter from my son Landon, the most affectionate and dutiful that could possibly be. At the same time one from John Carter, the mere hero among the brutes if not an Agent of Hell, the most

insulting, and false accusing letter that ever father had from a Son. I see clearly this Youth Misconstrues his father's long Patience under the barbarous ill treatment of his eldest son, Not considering who has forbid the Alienation of the Inheritance of their fathers. Religion may restrain me from Punishment in a case where God alone has by way of Promise implied the mode of his Punishment in the 5 Commandment. But when I give what was not the inheritance of my father but of my own requisition I see no religion to restrain my Punishing such a [barbarous] treatment to a father. Therefore, I shall tell him I will answer his letter in my Will where I shall record it to bid defiance to him and all this world to make good one Charge against me. Such language could only be derived from the Gaming table where self and gain alone Govern, at the Sacrifice of every duty, whether Moral or religious.

11 August. Hot and dry. If indolence, sleeping, Pleasure, and gaming can preserve an estate, My Son R. may keep what he has even in the worst of times. If insulting a grandfather, Storming at a mother, being angry and Outrageous at younger Sisters; Only loving a horse so much as always to have him in sight, tied at one Slender gate, or feeding before his window to break everything not his own to pieces; Dogs all around him, in his bedchamber and before his door, till he chuses a more orderly room, to fill with flies and ticks, can denot a gentle man of Politeness, Landon, the son of the aforesaid R, is certainly the highest bread youth on earth. Add to his insult, his seizing his Grandfather, laughing at his father, and with great injustice severely chastizing a servant not his own, whilst he protects the laziness of his own, even to a degree of the greatest filial disobedience. In short, he is as near in dirt and dress, to the famous Hastings as Possible. Hardly a breath of air now many days.

Formal schooling in the colonial South was less common than in the North, largely because plantation agriculture was not conducive to the growth of towns. The education of children went on nonetheless. Among the gentry tutors hired from the nearest college or as indentured servants from England often taught the children of one or more families on the plantation itself. The following documents reveal the daily activities of these young men. The first is The Journal of John Harrower, An Indentured Servant in the Colony of Virginia,

1773-1776, *edited by Edward Miles Riley for Colonial Williamsburg in 1963. The second is a letter of advice from a young graduate of Princeton to a friend and classmate who was about to succeed him as tutor to the children of Robert Carter in Virginia. It is taken from the* Journal & Letters of Philip Vickers Fithian, 1773-1774: A Plantation Tutor of the Old Dominion, *edited by Hunter Dickinson Farish (Williamsburg, 1943), pp. 208-222.*

Wednesday, 26th. [January 1774] This day I being reduced to the last shilling I hade was obliged to engage to go to Virginia for four years as a schoolmaster for Bedd, Board, washing and five pound during the whole time. I have also wrote my wife this day a particular Accot of everything that has happned to me since I left her untill this date; At 3 pm this day I went on board the Snow Planter Capt Bowers Comr for Virginia now lying at Ratliff Cross, and imediatly as I came Onbd I recd my Hammock and Bedding. at 4 pm came Alexr Steuart onbd the same Ship. he was Simbisters Servt and had only left Zetland about three weeks before. . . .

SUNDAY 6TH. [February 1774]

At 7 AM got under way with a fair wind and clear wr. [weather] and at 11 AM came to an anchor off Gravesend and immediately the Mercht. came on board and a Doctor & clerk with him and while the Clerk was fulling up the Indentures the doctor search'd every servt. to see that they were sound when two was turned ashore haveing the clap, and Seventy five were Intend to Capt. Bowres for four Years.

MUNDAY 7TH. FEBY. 1774

This forenoon imployed in getting in provisions and water; at 4 pm put a servant ashore extreamly bade in a fiver, and then got under saile for Virginia with seventy Servants on board all indented to serve four years there at their differint Occupations myself being one of the Number and Indented for a Clerk and Bookeeper, But when I aravied there I cou'd get no such birth as will appear in its place. At pm we came to an anchor at the Nore it blowing and snowing verry hard.

Freiday 13th. [May] This forenoon put ashore here what bale goods we hade remaining onboard. in the afternoon Mr. Burnet, Stewart and myself went ashore on liberty to take a walk and see the Toun, who's principal street is about half an English Mile long, the houses generally at a little distance one from another, some of them being built of wood and some of them of brick, and all covered with wood in the form of sclates about four Inches broad, which when painted blue you wou'd not know it from a house sclated with Isedell sclate. In this Toun the Church, the Counsell house, the Tolbooth the Gallows and the Pillory are all within 130 yds of each other. The Market house is a large brick Building a litle way from the Church. here we drank some Bottles of beer of their own brewing and some bottles of Cyder for which we paid 3-1/2 per bottle of each. returned on board in the evening. Turner still in handcuffs.

Munday 16th. This day severalls came onbd to purchase servts Indentures and among them there was two Soul drivers. they are men who make it their business to go onbd all ships who have in either Servants or Convicts and buy sometimes the whole and sometimes a parcell of them as they can agree, and then they drive them through the Country like a percell of Sheep untill they can sell them to advantage, but all went away without buying any.

Tuesday 17th. This day Mr Anderson the Mercht sent for me into the (cabin) and verry genteely told me that on my recomendations he would do his outmost to get me settled as a Clerk or bookeeper if not as a schoolmaster which last he told me he thought wou'd turn out more to my advantage upon being settled in a good famely . . .

Munday 23d. This morning a great number of Gentlemen and Ladies driving into Town it being an annuall Fair day and tomorrow the day of the Horse races. at 11 AM Mr Anderson begged to settle as a schoolmaster with a friend of his one Colonel Dangerfield and told me he was to be in Town tomorrow, or perhaps tonight, and how soon he came he shou'd acquant me. at same time all the rest of the servants were ordred ashore to a tent at Fredericksbg and severall of their Indentures were then sold. about 4 pm I was brought to Colonel Daingerfield, when we immediately agreed and my Indenture for four years was then delivered him and he was to send for me the next day. at same time ordred to get all my dirty Cloaths of every kind washed at his expense in Toun; at night he sent me five shillings onbd by Capt Bowers to keep my pocket.

Tuesday 24th. This morning I left the Ship at 6 AM having been sixteen weeks and six days on board her. I hade for Breackfast after I came ashore one Chappin sweet milk for which I paid 3-1/2 Cury at 11 AM went to see a horse race about a mille from Toun, where there was a number of Genteel Company as well as others. here I met with the Colonel again and after some talk with him he gave me cash to pay for washing all my Cloaths and something over. The reace was gain'd by a Bay Mare, a white boy ridder. There was a gray Mare started with the Bay a black boy ridder but was far distant the last heat.

Wednesday 25th. I Lodged in a Tavern last night and paid 7-1/2 for my Bedd and 7-1/2 for my breakfast. this morning a verry heavy rain untill 11 AM. Then I recd my Linens &c. all clean washed and packing every thing up I went onboard the ship and Bought this Book for which I paid 18d. Str. I also bought a small Divinity book called the Christian Monitor and a spelling book, both at 7-1/2 and an Arithmetick at 1/6d. all for my Accot.

Thursday 26th. This day at noon the Colonel sent a Black with a cuple of Horses for me and soon after I set out on Horseback and aravied at his seat of Belvidera about 3 pm and after I hade dined the Colonel took me to a neat little house at the upper end of an Avenue of planting at 500 yd from the Main house, where I was to keep the school, and Lodge myself in it.

This place is verry pleasantly situated on the Banks of the River Rappahannock about seven miles below the Toun of Fredericksburgh and the school's right above the Warff so that I can stand in the door and pitch a stone onboard of any ship or Boat going up or coming doun the river.

Freiday 27th. This morning about 8 AM the Colonel delivered his three sons to my Charge to teach them to read write and figure. his oldest son Edwin 10 years of age, intred into two syllables in the spelling book, Bathourest (Bathurst) his second son six years of age in the Alphabete and William his third son 4 years of age does not know the letters. he has likeways a Daughter whose name is Hanna Basset   Years of age. Soon after we were all sent for to breackfast to which we hade tea, Bread, Butter and cold meat and there was at table the Colonel, his Lady, his Children, the housekeeper and myself. At 11 AM the Colonel and his Lady went some where to pay a visit, he upon horseback and she in her Charriot. At 2 pm I dined with the Housekeeper the Children and a stranger Lady. at 6 pm I left school, and then I eat plenty of fine strawberries, but they neither drink Tea in the afternoon nor eat any supper here for the most part. My school Houres is from 6 to 8 in the morning, in the forenoon from 9 to 12 and from 3 to 6 in the afternoon . . .

Wednesday June 1st. This day there was prayers in all the Churches in Virginia on Accot of the disagreement at present betwixt great Brittain and her Colonies in North America, On Accot of their not agreeing to pay a duty on Tea laid on them by the british parliament and the Bostonians destroying a Quantity of Tea belonging to the British East India Compy in 1773 . . .

Saturday 11th. At 9 AM left the school and went a fishing on the River with the Colonel his eldest (Son) and another Gentleman in two Canoes, Mrs. Dangerfield another Lady and the other two boys mett us at Snow Creek in the Chair at 2 pm when we all dined on fish under a tree.

Sunday 12th. This day at Church at Fredericksburgh and at same time settled a Correspondance at Glasgow for getting letters from home, by their being put under cover to Messrs. Anderson and Horsburgh Merchts in Do and the expence charged to Mr. Glassel Mercht in Fredericksbg Virginia.

Tuesday 14th. This morning entred to school William Pattie son to John Pattie wright, and Salley Evens daughter to Thomas Evens Planter. This day I wrote my wife a particular Accot of all my transactions since I wrote her from London 26th Jany last, the Coppy of which I have by me . . .

Munday 20th. This morning entred to school Philip and Dorothea Edge's Children of Mr Benjaman Edge Planter . . .

Tuesday 21st. This day Mr Samuel Edge Planter came to me and begged me to take a son of his to school who was both deaf and dum, and I consented to try what I cou'd do with him . . .

Thursday 23d. This day entred to school John Edge son to the above named Mr Sam: Edge, he is a lad about 14 years of age and is both deaf and dum.

Saturday 25th. This afternoon I went and took a walk in the wheat field and under a tree I filled all my pockets of as fine walnuts as ever I eat, But so hard shell that I was oblidged to have a hammer to breack them.

Sunday 26th. After Breackfast I took a walk 3 Miles to Mr. Edge's, the dum lad's father where I dined and drank some grogg and returned home in the afternoon. at night I had a small Congregation of Negroes, learng their Catechisim and hearing me read to them.

Sunday July 3d. At home all the forenoon, in the afternoon went to see One Mr. Richards an Overseer and his wife where I eat plenty of honney out of the Comb, it being taken out of a Beehive in a tree in the woods last night.

Freiday 8th. After school houres I went two Miles to see the Taylor who made my Cloaths he being a Brittoner but married to a Buckskine, and I found his wife and Daughters drinking tea, at which I joyned them, The Taylor not being at home.

Tuesday 12th. Sold the spelling book that I bought Onbd the Planter 25th May last, and got the same money for it that I paid for the Christian Monitor and it.

Saturday 16th. This afternoon the Colonel finished the cutting down of His wheat which cost of wages to hired people £ 23: 10 Curry besides their victualls and drink.

Munday 18th. This morning entred to School Lewis Richards. Same day I put on a pair of new shoes made in Fredericksburgh of English calf leather the price of them 12/6 Curry. Same day gave one pair of old worsted stockins for 22 foot of Gum plank 10 Inch broad and one thick to make me a Chest.

Tuesday 19th. On Freiday 15th, Inst John Edge the Dum lad left the school at 6 pm and has not returned since.

Wednesday 20th. On Munday 4th, Inst at 6 pm William Pattie left the school and has not returned since.

Munday 25th. Nothing remarkable. Jno Edge returnd to school . . .

Belvidera 14th June 1774.

My Dearest Life

I wrote you from London on Wednesday 26th Jany last which Im hopefull came safe to hand, and found you and my dear Infants in perfect health, and am hopefull this will find both you and them in the same state, As I am at present and have been I bless God since I left you. You will remember when I wrote you last, I informed you that I was to go for Baltimore in Maryland. But I altred my design in that and came here it being a more healthy pleace. I sailed from London on Freiday the 4th Feby last, and arrived in Hampton roads in Virginia on the 27 April, having been a Month of the time at Spithead in England. As to particulars of our Voyage &ca it would take up too much room here to insert it. But I have a Journal of every days transactions and remarcable Occurrances since the morning I left you which will be amusing to you when please God we are spared to meet, for I design to see and prepare a way for you all in this Country how soon I am able.—I shall now aquant you wt my situation in this Country. I am now settled with on Colonel Wm Dangerfield Esqr of Belvidera, on the Banks of the River Rappahannock about 160 miles from the Capes or sea mouth, and seven Miles below the Toun of Fredericksburgh. My business is to teach his Children to read write and figure, Edwin his oldest son about 8 years of (age) Bathurest his second 6 years of age and William his youngest son 4 years of age. He has also a Daughter whose name is Hanna Basset. I came to this place on Thursday 26th May and next morning I received his three sons into my charge to teach, the two youngest boys I got in A:B:C. and the oldest Just begun to syllab and I have now the two youngest spelling and the oldest reading. I am obliged to teach in the English method which was a little aquard [awkward] to me at first but now quite easy. I am also obliged to talk english the best I can, for Lady Dangerfield speacks nothing but high english, and the Colonel hade his Education in England and is a verry smart Man. As to my agreement it is as follows Vizt I am obliged to continue with Col. Dangerfield for four years if he insists on it, and for teaching his own children I have Bed, Board, washing and all kind of Cloaths during the above time, and for what schoolars I can get more than his Children I have five shillings currency per Quarter for each of them, which is equall to four shillings sterling, and I expect ten or twelve to school next week, for after I had been here eight days and my abilities and my behavior sufficiently tried, the Colonel rode through the neighbouring Gentlemen and Planters in order to procure scollars for me, so that I hope in a short time to make something of it. And as I have no Occasion to spend a farthing on myself every shillg I make shall be carefully remitted you, for your support and my Dear Infants. But I must be some time here before any thing can be done, for you know every thing must have a beginning.

As to my living I eat at their own table, and our witualls are all Dressed in the English taste. we have for Breackfast either Coffie or Jaculate [chocolate], and warm Loaf bread of the best floor, and we have also at table warm loaf bread of Indian corn, which is extreamly good but we use the floor bread always at breackfast. for Dinner smoack'd bacon or what we cal pork ham is a standing dish either warm or cold. when warm we have greens with it, and when cold we have sparrow grass. we have also either warm roast pigg, Lamb, Ducks, or chickens, green pease or any thing else they fancy. As for Tea there is none drunk by any in this Government since 1st June last, nor will they buy a 2ds worth of any kind of east India goods, which is owing to the difference at present betwixt the Parliment of great Britton and the North Americans about laying a tax on the tea; and I'm afraid if the Parliment do not give it over it will cause a total revolt as all the North Americans are determined to stand by one another, and resolute on it that they will not submit. I have the news paper sent me to school regularly every week by the Coll.—Our family consists of the Coll his Lady and four Children a housekeeper an Overseer and myself all white. But how many blacks young and old the Lord only knows for I belive there is about thirty that works every day in the field besides the servants about the house; such as Gardner, livery men and pages, Cooks, washer and dresser, sewster and waiting girle. They wash here the whitest that ever I seed for they first Boyle all the Cloaths with soap, and then wash them, and I may put on clean linen every day if I please. My schoole is a neate litle House 20 foot long and 12 foot wide and it stands by itself at the end of an Avenue of planting about as far from the main house as Robt Forbes's is from the burn, and there comes a bonny black bairn every morning to clean it out and make my bed, for I sleep in it by myself. I have a verry fine feather bed under me, and a pair of sheets, a thin fold of a Blanket and a Cotton bed spread is all by bed cloaths, and I find them just enough. as for myself I suppose you wou'd scarce know me now, there being nothing either brown, blew, or black about me but the head and feet, I being Dressed in short cloath Coat, vest Coat, and britches all made of white cotton without any lyning and thread stockins and wearing my own hair curled round like a wigg. at present a suite of Cloaths costs five and twenty shillings here of making which I really think verry high.

I was Sunday last at Fredericksburgh at church and I then settled a safe Correspondance for your letters to come to me, and shall give you the proper directions below. As for myself I thank God I want for nothing that is necessary, But it brings tears from my eyes to think of you and my infants when at the same time it is not in my power at present to help you. But how soon I am able you may depend upon it. I have litle else to say at present; only may the great

God who governs all things wisely suport you and my Infants, and guide and direct you in all your ways.

I shall write you again soon and when you write me direct my letters as follows Vizt to John Harrower at the seat of Colonel Wm Dangerfield Esqr of Belvidera near Fredericksburgh on Rappahannock River Virginia; Then you must take half a sheet of paper and write another letter the contents of which may be as follows Vizt Gentlemen, being dcsired by my husband to send his letters under cover to you, You will please forward the inclosed by the first ship bound for any part in Virginia and charge Mr Glassel Mercht in Fredericksburgh with the expence you are at; I am yours &c Signed A. H. After you have closed my letter and directed it as above, You will inclose it in the above, and direct it as follows To Messrs Anderson and Horsburgh Merchts in Glasgow. You must get some person to fold up your letter properly and on[e] who writes a clear Distinct hand to direct them. Pray write me verry particularly how it is with you and my Dr Infants, likeways any thing that is remarcable in the Country. I shall conclude this with offering my Compts to all enquiring freinds if I have any and my sinceer prayers both evening and morng for you and my Children. My Blessing to you all, is all at prsent from my Dearest Jewell your ever affte Husband untill Death. Signed, John Harrower.

Addressed, To Mrs. John Harrower in Lerwick, Zetland . . .

Wednesday 17th. [August] This evening entred to school Thomas Brooks Mr Spotswoods carpenter in order to learn Writing and Arithmetick at nights and on Sundays . . .

Sunday 28th. At home all day teaching Brooks.

Sunday September 11th. Do [ditto]. teaching Brooks. at 1 pm came Mr Kennedy from Fredericksburgh here to see me and after we had dined we ended the Quart of Rum I bought 16th Last Mo.

Tuesday October 4th. Went to Fredericksbg and seed a Horse Race for a Hundred Guineas, Gained by Mr Fitchews Horse . . .

Belvidera 6th Decr 1774.

My Dearest Life . . .

I have as yet only ten scollars One of which is both Deaff and Dumb and his Father pays me ten shilling per Quarter for him he has been now five Mos with (me) and I have brought him tolerably well and understands it so far, that he can write mostly for anything he wants and understands the value of every figure and can work single addition a little. he is about fourteen years of age. Another of them is a young man a house Carpenter who attends me every night with candle light and every Sunday that I don't go to Church for which he pays me fourty shillings a year. He is Carpenter for a gentleman who lives two miles from me and has Thirty pound a year, free bedd and board.

The Colls Children comes on pretty well. the Eldest is now reading verry distinctly in the Psalter according to the Church of England and the other two boys ready to enter into it; the Coll and his Lady being extreamly well satisfied wt my Conduct in every respect; On 31st Jully last Mrs Dangerfield was delivd of a fourth son who is now my nameson . . .

I yet hope please God, if I am spared, some time to make you a Virginian Lady among the woods of America which is by far more pleasant than the roaring of the raging seas round abo't Zetland. And yet to make you eat more wheat Bread in your old age than what you have done in your Youth. But this I must do by carefullness, industry and a Close Application to Business, which ye may take notice of in this letter I am doing Sunday as well as Saturday nor will I slip an honest method nor an hour whereby I can gain a penny for yours and my own advantage . . .

Sunday 25th. Christmas day, stayed at home all day along wt the Overseer and Children because I hade no saddle to go to the Church with. In the morning the Coll Ordred up to school two Bottles of the best Rum and some suggar for me.

Munday 26th. This forenoon the Coll wou'd have me to take his saddle and ride to Toun and Amuse myself, and when I was going gave me Six Shillings for pocket money. I went to Toun and Dined in a private house and after buying 1-1/2 Dozn Mother of Pearle buttons for my white morsyld Vest I return'd home in the evening.

Tuesday 27th. St. John's day. This day a Grand Lodge in Toun, And the whole went to Church in their Clothing and heard sermon.

Thursday 29th. I began to keep school.

Freiday 30th. This day there was severall Gentlemen from Fredericksburgh here at Dinner with whom I dined.

Tuesday January 10th, 1775. This day Thos Brooks who has atten(d) ed ever night and on Sundays left school being obliged to go 40 miles up the country to work. at same time he gave me an order on Coll Daingerfield for £1. 10. 8. Curry of which £1. 5. 2 was for teaching him . . .

Tuesday 31st. 1 pm yesterday Jas and Wm Porters, sons of Mr William Porter Mercht in Fredericksbg came here to School . . .

Munday 27th. This day Mr Fraser came here and entred to take his charge as Overseer, and he is to have his bed in the school along with me. he appears to be a verry quiet young man and has hade a tolerable education. his Grandfather came from Scotland . . .

Saturday 25th. At noon went to Newport to see Mr Martin Heely schoolmaster to Mr Spotswood's Children, and after Dinner I spent the afternoon with him in conversation and hearing him play the Fiddle. He also made a Niger come and play on an Instrument call'd a Barrafou . . .

Saturday April 1st. At 6 pm Mr Martin Heely schoolmaster at Newport for Mr Spotswoods Children came here to pay me a Visite and staid with me all night.

Sunday 9th. This day a good number of Company dined here among which was Mr and Mrs Porter from Town, who heard their eldest son read and seemed verry well pleased with his performance since he came to me: Myself at home all day.

Freiday 14th. This being good Frieday, I broke up school for Easter Holly day, and the Colls three sons went to Town with Mr Porter's two sons this forenoon I went a money hunting but catc'd none . . .

Thursday 20th. This morning all the boys came to school again at their Usual hour . . .

Sunday 7th. [May] At 2 houses this day seeking money that was owing me but got none . . .

Saturday June 3d. At 9 AM Mr Porter's two son's was sent for and they went to Toun to keep Whitsuntide holliday . . .

Wednesday 19th. [July] This day I was Informed that Mrs Daingerfield hade made a Complaint upon me to the Colo for not waiting after Breackfast and dinner (sometimes) in order to take the Children along with me to scholl; I imagine she has a grudge against me since the middle of Feby last the reason was, that one night in the Nursery I wheep'd Billie for crying for nothing and she came in and carried him out from me. Some nights after he got into the same humour and his Papa The Colo hearing him call'd me and Asked why I cou'd hear him do so and not correct him for it; Upon that I told him how Mrs Daingerfield had behaved when I did correct him. At that he was angry wt her . . .

Sunday 23d. Mrs Porter having been here all night from Town; I this day after breackfast brought all the boys with their books into the passage to the Colo who heard each of them read and was highly pleased with their performance. Mrs Porter likeways told that her sons did me great honour; as well as the rest . . .

Wednesday August 2d. This day came to School Wm John and Lucy Patties, and are to pay conform to the time they attend . . .

Munday 28th. [August] Coppy of my 4th Letter wrote this day to my wife.

My Dearest Life . . .

About 7 months ago a Gentleman in Fredericksbg hade his two sons taken from the high school there and put under my care for which he pays me £5 a year. He is an English man himself and his Lady from Edinburgh, and I have the pleasure to have given the parents such satisfaction that I hade sent me in a present two silk vestcoats and two pairs of britches ready to put on for changes in summer. I observe my Dear Dogg George writes me his name at the foot of your letter, But I am surprized that you take no notice of Jack and Bettie. But I hope you will not faill to be more particular about them in your next, and give my blessing to them all and tell them from me that I hope they will be obedient to you in every respect and mind their books . . .

Wednesday 6th. [September 1775]. This day I was informed by Mr Frazer that Mrs Daingerfield talking to them of me that morning about some Glue disresptfully calld me Old Harrower by which and her behaveiour to myself I find her grudge continous tho she has not courage to say any thing to myself well knowing she has (no) foundation to go upon.

Sunday 10th. This day came Dick a Servt belonging to Mr Anderson from Toun and a Comerade of his to see me and Brought me a pair new shoes and a pair for Mr Frazer also a Bottle Vest India Rum which we drank in school in Company with Mr Frazer.

Thursday 28th. This morning I recd from Benjamin Edge by the hand of his daughter two Dollars, one half and one Quarter Dollar being in all sixteen shillings and Sixpence in part payment for teaching his son and daughter.

Thursday October 12th. Company here last night Vizt Old Mrs Waller, her son and his wife and at school there Mr Heely Schoolmaster and Mr Brooks Carpenter and they wt Mr Frazer and myself played whist and danced untill 12 OClock, Mr Heely the Fidle and dancing. We drank one bottle of rum in time. Mr Frazer verry sick after they went home.

Saturday 28th. Last night came here to school Mr Heely and Thos Brooks in order to spend the evening, but by reason of Mr Frazer's not coming from the House, and some stories told them by Mrs Richards in order to sow disention, She being really a Wolf cloathed with a lambs skin and the greatest Mischief maker I have seen in all my Travels, The first time I seed her, I cou'd observe in her countenance Slyness and deceit, and I have always avoided going to the House as much as possible, But now I really think she ought to be avoided by every christian who regairds peace and their own character, They both went home at 10 pm.

Wednesday January 10th, 1776. This day we hade the Confirmation of Norfolk being reduced to ashes by the Men of War and British Troops under Command of Lord Dunmore. It was the Largest Toun in the Collony and a place of great Trade, it being situated a little within the Capes. Severall Women and Childn are killed.

Tuesday 23. This day I entred Edwin into the Latin Gramer.

Tuesday March 5th. This morning Bathurest Daingerfield got don reading through the Bible and the new testament, and began to learn to write 15 Ulto I gave them Holyday this Afternoon.

Saturday April 20th. At noon I asked the Colo for a bottle of rum as I expected two Countrymen to see me tomorrow, which he verry cheerfully gave and desired me to ask him for one any time I wanted it and told me to take them to the Howse to dinner with me. in the afternoon he, his Lady, and Daughter went over the river to Mr Jones's in King George County.

Sunday 28th. This day came here to pay me a visit Mr Reid from Mansfield and Mr Scott from Toun and dined with me in the great house by the Colos order, and after we hade spent the afternoon verry agreeably together they returned home in the evening.

Sunday May 5th. Early this morning I went to Mr McCalley's and entred his oldest son (about 8 years of age) to writting, stayed there all day and rode his horse home in the evening. The Colo went to Newport and dinned there.

Tuesday 7th. Billie ended reading through his Bible.

Thursday 9th. After dinner I took the boys with me to Massaponacks Briges to see 56 prisoners that was taken at the late battle in North Carolina, among them was a great many Emigrants from Scotland who were all officers. I talked with several of them from Ross Shr and the Isle of Sky.

Thursday June 6th. In the afternoon I went to Mr Becks, when he told me that Mrs Battle wanted to see me and to talk to me about teaching her two daughters to write, upon which I imediately waited upon her and engaged to return upon Saturd next by 1 pm and begin them to write but made no bargain as yet.

Saturday 8th. At noon I went to Mrs Bataile's and entred two of her Daughters to writing, Viz. Miss Sallie and Miss Betty and continoued teaching them until night, when I agreed to attend them every Saturday afternoon and every other Sunday from this date until 8th June 1777 (If it please God to spare me) for four pound Virginia currancy.

Sunday 9th. After breackfast I rode to Mr McAlleys and teach'd his son to write untill 4 pm and then came home in the evening.

Wednesday 19th. At noon went to snow creek and the boys and dined at the spring on Barbaque and fish. At 5 pm I went to Mrs Bataile, and teac'd until 1/2 an hour past 7.

Wednesday 10th. At 6 pm went to Mrs Battaile's and teach'd untill sunset and then return'd home and soon after hea(r)d a great many guns fired towards Toun. about 12 pm the Colo Despatched Anthy Frazer there to see what was the cause of (it) who returned, and informed him that there was great rejoicings in Toun on Accot of the Congress having declared the 13 United Colonys of North America Independent of the Crown of great Britain.

                            Nomini Hall August 12th 1774.
                                "Si bene moneo, attende."—

Sir.

    I never reflect, but with secret, and peculiar pleasure, on the time when I studied in *Deerfield* with you, & several other pleasant Companions, under our common, & much respected instructor, Mr. *Green*.

And I acknowledge now, with a thankful heart, the many favours, which I received from your family while I was a member of it. This sense of obligation to your Family, And personal friendship for you, have excited me, when it was in my power, to introduce you to the business which I now occupy; into a family, where, if you be prudent and industrious, I am confident you will speedily acquire to yourself both Honour & Profit—But inasmuch as you are wholly a stranger to this Province; & have had little or no Experience in the business which you ar shortly to enter upon; & lest, from common Fame, which is often erroneous, you shall have entertained other notions of the manners of the People here, & of your business as a Tutor, than you will find, when you come, to be actually true; I hope you will not think it *vain* or *untimely*, if I venture to lay before you some Rules for your direction which I have collected from a year's observation. I shall class what I have to say in the following order. First. I shall attempt to give you some direction for the plan of your Conduct among your neighbours, & the People in General here, so long as you sustain the character of a Tutor. Then I shall advise you concerning the rules which I think will be most profitable & convenient in the management of your little lovely charge, the School. Last of all. I shall mention several Rules for your personal conduct. I choose to proceed in the order I have laid down, as well that you may more fully & speedily receive my mind, as that you may also the more readily select out and apply what you shall find to be most necessary.

First. When you have thought of removinging, for a Time, out of the Colony in which you was born, & in which you have hitherto constantly resided, I make no doubt but you have at the same time expected to find a very considerable alteration of manners, among your new acquaintances, & some peculiarities toto Caelo different, from any you have before been accustomed to. Such a thought is natural; And you will if you come into Virginia, in much shorter time than a year be convinced that it is just. In New-Jersey Government throughout, but especially in the Counties where you have any personal acquaintance, Gentlemen in the first rank of Dignity & Quality, of the Council, general Assembly, inferior Magistrates, Clergy-Men, or independent Gentlemen, without the smallest fear of bringing any manner of reproach either on their office, or their high-born, long recorded Families associate freely & commonly with Farmers & Mechanicks tho' they be poor & industrious. Ingenuity & industry are the Strongest, & most approved recommendations to a Man in that Colony. The manners of the People seem to me, (probably I am overborn by the force of prejudice in favour of my native Soil), to bear some considerable resemblance of the manners in the ancient Spartan Common-Wealth—The Valour of its Inhabitants—was the best, & only security of that State against the enemy; & the wise laws of its renowned Legislator were the powerful Cement which kept them firm & invincible—In our Government, the laborious part of Men, who are commonly ranked in the midling or lower Class, are accounted the strenth &Honor of the Colony; & the encouragement they receive from Gentlemen in the highest stations is the spring of Industry, next to their private advantage. The Level which is admired in New-Jersey Government, among People of every rank, arises, no doubt, from the very great division of the lands in that Province, & consequently from the near approach to an equality of Wealth amongst the Inhabitants, since it is not famous for trade. You know very well that the Lands in a small township are divided, & then again subdivided into two & three Hundred Separate, proper, creditable estates; for example *Deerfield* & Fairfield two Townships, or Precincts, in which you & I are tolerably well acquainted, in the former of which, are the Seats of two Judges of the Sessions; & in the latter resides one of the representatives in General Assembly for the County; But if 16000 £ would purchase the whole landed estates of these three Gentlemen, who are supposed to be the most wealthy in the County, if we rate their Land at the Low Consideration of 4L p acre, with all conveniences, each would have 4000 Acres. Now you may suppose how small a quantity many must have when two or three hundred Landholders reside in each of these small Precincts; Hence we see Gentlemen, when they are not actually engaged in the publick Service, on their farms, setting a laborious example to their Domesticks, & on the other hand we see labourers at the Tables & in the Parlours of their Betters enjoying the advantage, & honor of their society and Conversation—I do not call it an objection to this, that some few, who have no substance but work like Slaves as necessity drives them for a few Months in the year; with the price of this Labour they visit Philadelphia; & having there acquired a fashionable Coat, & a Stock of Impudence, return home to spend the remainder of the year, in idleness & disgrace!—But you will find the tables turned the moment you enter this Colony. The very Slaves, in some families here, could not be bought under 30000 £. Such amazing property, no matter how deep it is involved, blows up the owners to an imagination, which is visible in all, but in various degrees according to their respective virtue, that they are exalted as much above other Men in worth & precedency, as blind stupid fortune has made a difference in their property; excepting always the value they put upon posts of honour, & mental acquirements—For example, if you should travel through this Colony, with a well-confirmed testimonial of your having finished with Credit a Course of studies at Nassau-Hall; you would be rated, without any more questions asked, either about your family, your Estate, your business, or your intention, at 10,000 £; and you might come, & go, & converse, & keep company, according to this value; & you would be dispised & slighted if yo(u) rated yourself a farthing cheaper. But when I am giving directions to you, from an expectation that you will be shortly a resident here, altho you have gone through a College Course, & for any thing I know, have never written a Libel, nor stolen a Turkey, yet I think myself in duty bound to advise you, lest some powdered Coxcomb should reproach your education, to cheapen your price about 5000 £; because any young Gentleman travelling through the Colony, as I said before, is presum'd to be acquainted with Dancing, Boxing, playing the Fiddle, Small-Sword, & Cards. Several of which you was only entering upon, when I left New-Jersey; towards the Close of last year; and if you stay here any time your Barrenness in these must be detected. I will however allow, that in the Family where you act as tutor you place yourself, according to your most accute Calculation, at a perfect equidistance between the father & the eldest Son. Or let the same distance be observed in every article of behaviour between you & the eldest Son, as there ought to be, by the latest & most approved precepts of Moral-Philosophy, between the eldest Son, & his next youngest Brother. But whenever you go from Home, where you are to act on your own footing, either to a Ball; or to a *Horse-Race*, or to a *Cock-Fight*, or to a *Fish-Feast*, I advise that you rate yourself very low, & if you bet at all, remember that 10,000 £ in Reputation & learning does not amount to a handfull of Shillings in ready Cash!—Once considerable advantage which you promise yourself by coming to this Colony is to extend the Limits of your acquaintance; this is laudable, & if you have enough of prudence & firmness, it will be of singular advantage—Yet attempt slowly & with the most Jealous Circumspection—If you fix your familiarity wrong in a single instance, you are in danger of total, if not immediate ruin—You come here, it is true, with an intention to teach, but you ought likewise to have an inclination to learn. At any rate I solemnly injoin it upon you, that you never suffer the spirit of a Pedagogue to attend you without the walls of your little Seminary. In all promiscuous Company be as silent & attentive as Decency will allow you, for you have nothing to communicate, which such company, will hear with pleasure, but you may learn many things which, in after life, will do you singular service.—In regard to Company in general, if you think it worth the while to attend to my example, I can easily instruct you in the manner of my Conduct in this respect. I commonly attend Church; and often, at the request of Gentlemen, after Service according to the custom, dine abroad on Sunday—I seldom fail, when invited by Mr or Mrs *Carter*, of going out with them; but I make it a point, however strongly solicited to the contrary, to return home with them too—Except in one of these cases, I seldom go out, but with a valuable variety of books I live according to Horace's direction, & love "Secretum Iter et fallentis Semita Vitae." Close retirement and a life by Stealth. The last direction I shall venture to mention on this head, is, that you abstain totally from Women. What I would have you understand from this, is, that by a train of faultless conduct in the whole course of your tutorship, you make every Lady within the Sphere of your acquaintance, who is between twelve & forty years of age, so much pleased with your person, & so fully satisfied as to your abilities in the capacity of—a Teacher; & in short, fully convinced, that, from a principle of Duty, you have, both by night & by day endeavoured to acquit yourself honourably, in the Character of a Tutor; & that, on this account, you have their free & hearty consent, without making any manner of demand upon you, either to stay longer in the County with them, which they would choose, or whenever your business calls you away, that they may not have it in their Power either by charms or Justice to detain you, when you must leave them, have their sincere wishes & constant prayrs for Length of days & much prosperity, I therefore beg that you will attend litterally to this advice, & abstain totally from Women. But this last precaution, which I have been at some pains to dress in the plainest language, I am much inclined to think, will be wholly useless in regard to you, notwithstanding it is founded in that *Honour* and *Equity* which is on all hands allow'd to be due from one Sex to the other, & to many of your *age*, & Standing no doubt would be entirely salutary. Because the necessary connections which you have had with the Fair, from your Puberty upwards have been so un-

favourable & ill-fated, that instead of apprehending any danger on the score of over fondness, I am fearful your rancour has grown so inveterate at length, as, not only to preserve you, in thought & practice, pure of every Fleshly foible, but has carried you so far towards the other extream, as that you will need many persuasions, when your circumstances shall seem to require it, to bring you back to a rational & manly habit of thinking & acting with respect to the Sex; which yet, after all (& eternally will continue to be, tho it is much courted & whined after) if considered in the fullest manner, & set forth to the best advantage, never rises above its divine definition Viz "The weaker Vessel." But without detaining you any longer with a matter merely depending on accident or Circumstance I pass on to the second General Head; in which "Ludis atque Jocis amotis" I shall offer to your consideration & recommend for your practice several Rules concerning the management of the School.
2. You will act wisely, if, from the begining, you convince all your Scholars which you may easily do, of your abilities in the several branches, which you shall profess to teach; you are not to tell them, totidem Verbis, "that you understand, perhaps as well as any man on the Continent both the Latin & Greek Classicks"; "& have gone through the usual Course in the noted College of New-Jersey, under Dr Witherspoon, so universally known & admired, where you have studied Criticism, Oratory, History, not to mention Mathematical & philosophical Studies, & dipt a good way into the French-Language, & that you have learn'd a smattering of Dancing, Cards &c. &c. &c."
For Dun-p or Hack-n or the most profound dunce in your College or School would have too much sense to pass such impudence by, & not despise and reproach it; but you may speedily & certainly make them think you a "Clever Fellow" (which is a phrase in use here for a good Scholar) if you never mention any thing before them, only what you seem to be wholly master of—This will teach them never to dispute your determination, & always to rely upon your Judgment; two things which are most essential for your peace, & their advantage. That you may avoid yourself of this with certainty I shall recommend for your practice the following method, as useful at least, if not intirely necessary. Read over carefully, the lessons in Latin & Greek, in your leisure hours, that the story & Language be fresh in your memory, when you are hearing the respective lessons; for your memory is treacherous, & I am pretty certain it would confound you if you should be accosted by a pert School-Boy, in the midst of a blunder,

with "Physician heal thyself"!—You ought likewise to do this with those who are working Figures; probably you may think that because the highest Cypher is only in decimal arithmetic, it is not there fore worth your critical attention to be looking previously into the several Sums. But you are to consider that a sum in the Square-Root, or even in the Single Rule of three direct, is to your Pupils of as great importance, as the most abstruse problem in the Mathematicks to an able artist; & you may lay this down for a Maxim, that they will reckon upon your abilities, according as they find you acquainted & expert in what they themselves are studying. If therefore you have resolution (as I do not question your ability) to carry this plan which I have laid down into execution; you will thereby convince them of the propriety of their Subordination to you, & obedience to your instructions, so that you may lead them, without any resistance, and fix them to the Study of whatever Science you think proper, in which they will rise according to their respective Capacities. I have said that you ought to strive "from the beginning" in fixing this very material article in the minds of your Scholars, Viz a Sense of your authority; for one error of Judgment, or false determination will diminish your Ability with them more than doing forty things with truth would increase your authority—They act in this case as you would do in the company of a number of Strangers—A whole evenings conversation, if it was tolerable good Sense, would perhaps make little or no impression on you; But if through hast in speaking, of inattention, any one should let fall a sentence either remarkably foolish, or grossly wicked, it would be difficult if not impossible to persuade you presently that the author was not either a *thick-Scull*, or a *Villain!*—The education of children requires constant unremitting attention. The meanest qualification you can mention in a useful teacher is *diligence* And without diligence no possible abilities or qualifications can bring children on either with speed or profit. There must be a Combination of qualifications which must all operate strongly & uniformly. In short, give this said Pedagogizing the softest name you will, it is still a "difficult Task." You will meet with numberless difficulties, in your new imployment, which you never dreamt had yet existence. All these you must endeavor to resist & Subdue. This I have seen compared to a Man swimming against a current of Water. But I am mistaken if you will agree, after having six months practice, that the comparison be strong as the truth: You will add to the figure, I am certain, & throw into the Current sharp fragments of

Ice, & Blocks, which would make swimming not only difficult but dangerous! I am not urging these things to discourage you; they are hints for your direction, which, if you will attend to, tho' at first the practice seem rough & unpleasant, shall yet make the remainder of your task pleasing, & the whole of it useful, I will mention several of these Obstacles that you may the more easily guard against them. You will, in the first place, be often solicited, probably oftner than you would wish, to ride abroad; this, however, if you do it moderately, & in seasonable time, & go to proper company, I recommend as conducive to health to one in your sedentary manner of living. But if you go much into company, you will find it extremely difficulty to break away with any manner of credit till very late at night or in most cases for several days, & if you are wanting to your School, you do manifest injury to your Imployer. In this case, I advise you to copy Mr *Carter*. Whenever he invites you, ride. You may *stay*, and talk, & drink, & ride to as great excess as he; & may with safety associate yourself with those whom you find to be his intimates. In all other Cases, except when you ride to Church, at least till you are very intimate in the Colony, you had better ride to a certain Stump, or to some noted plantation, or pretty landscape; you will have in this every advantage of exercise, the additional advantage of undisturbed meditation, & you will be under no Jealous apprehension in point of behaviour, nor any restraint as to the time of your return.

Another current difficulty will be petitions for holidays. You must have good deal of steadiness if you are able to evade cleverly this practice which has grown so habitual to your little charge from a false method in their early education that they absolutely claim it as a necessary right.

You must also as much as you can, avoid visible partiality. At least you must never suffer your fondness for one Scholar to grow so manifest, as that all your School shall see you look over a fault in him or her which same fault, if commited by another, you severely chastise. This will certainly produce in the others hatred & contempt. A fourth difficulty, and the last I shall mention, consists in knowing when, & in what measure to give the Boys Liberty to go from Home. The two younger Boys are wholly under your inspection; so that not only the progress they make in learning, but their moral Conduct (for both of these are critically observed & examined) either justifies or condemns your management to the World. If you keep them much at home, & close to business, they themselves will call you unfeeling and cruel; & refuse to be industrious; if you suffer them to go much abroad they are certainly out of the way of improvement by study, probably, by discovering their gross Ignorance, they will expose to ridicule both themselves & all their former instructors, & possibly they may commit actual Crimes so as very much to injure themselves; & scandalize their family; but in each of these you will have a large share of blame, perhaps more than the parents, or even the Boys themselves—It will be said that the parents gave them no licence relying wholly on your Judgment & prudence, this will in good measure Justify them to the world. And as to the Boys they are full of youthful impetuosity & vigour, & these compel them, when they are free of restraint, to commit actions which with proper management they had surely avoided. I say, when you lay these things together, & view them on every side you will find so many perplexities arising in your mind, from a sense of ignorance of your duty, that you will proceed with caution & moderation, & will be carefull to examine with some precision into the circumstances of *time, company,* & Business when you license them to go out entirely at the risk of your Reputation—But the practice of three or four Weeks will give you a more full notion of these & many other incidents that I am able now either to recollect or express; I shall have gained my End if these hints prevent you from setting off wrong, & doing inadvertantly at first what your Scholars will assert to be precedents for your after conduct. I go on, therefore, in the third place as I proposed,

3. To mention several Rules for your personal conduct. The happy Education which you have had in point of religion, you ought to consider as an important and distinguishing Blessing of Heaven. That train of useful *Instruction, Advice* & *Example* to which you have been accustomed from your infancy is a more perfect, & will be a safer guide in your future walk, than any directions I am able to give you. You have taken notice of a method for Assistance in Composition, which Longinus recommends.

Place, says he, in imagination, several eminent ancient Authors before your Eyes, & suppose that they inspect your Work, a Sense of Inferiority would make you diligent, & your composition accurate. Perhaps the same advice when transferr'd to Morality, would be equally salutary. Unless it be objected that a Belief of Gods presence at all times in every place is the strongest possible restraint against committing Sin. This I constantly admit; but when I consider how easily our minds are put in motion, & how strongly they are sometimes agitated merely by the senses, & that the senses are affected most by things which fall under their immediate notice, I am fully convinced that if some such plan as I have just mentioned should be fallen upon, & practised, it would make a visible and useful change in our behaviour—In this place I think it needful to caution you against hasty & ill founded prejudices. When you enter among a people, & find that their manner of living, their *Eating, Drinking,* Diversions, Exercise &c, are in many respects different from any thing you have been accustomed to, you will be apt to fix your opinion in an instant, & (as some divines deal with poor Sinners) you will condemn all before you without any meaning or distinction what seems in your Judgment disagreeable at first view, when you are smitten with the novelty. You will be making ten thousand Comparisons. The face of the Country, The *Soil*, the *Buildings*, the *Slaves*, the *Tobacco*, the method of spending *Sunday* among Christians; *Ditto* among the Negroes; the three grand divisions of time at the Church on Sundays, Viz. before Service giving & receiving letters of business, reading Advertisements, consulting about the price of Tobacco, Grain &c, & settling either the lineage, Age, or qualities of favourite Horses 2. In the Church at Service, prayrs read over in haste, a Sermon seldom under & never over twenty minutes, but always made up of sound morality, or deep studied Metaphysicks. 3. After Service is over three quarters of an hour spent in strolling round the Church among the Crowd, in which time you will be invited by several different Gentlemen home with them to dinner. The Balls, the Fish-Feasts, the Dancing-Schools, the Christnings, the Cock fights, the Horse-Races, the Chariots, the Ladies Masked, for it is a custom among the Westmorland Ladies whenever they go from home, to muffle up their heads, & Necks, leaving only a narrow passage for the Eyes, in Cotton or silk handkerchiefs; I was in distress for them when I first came into the Colony, for every Woman that I saw abroad, I looked upon as ill either with the *Mumps* or Tooth-Ach!—I say, you will be often observing & comparing these things which I have enumerated, & many more that now escape me, with the manner of spending Money time & credit at Cohansie: You are young, &, (you will allow me the Expression) in the morning of Life. But I hope you have plann'd off, and entered upon the work which is necessary to be performed in the course of your Day; if not, I think it my duty to acquaint you, that a combination of the amusements which I have just now mentioned, being always before your

Eyes, & inviting your Compliance will have a strong tendency to keep you doubtful & unsetled, in your notions of Morality & Religion, or else will fix you in a false & dangerous habit of *thinking & acting,* which must terminate at length in Sorrow & despair. You are therefore, if you count any thing upon the value of my advice, to fix the plan in which you would spend your life; let this be done with deliberation, Candour, & precission, looking to him for direction, by fervent Prayr, who is the "Wonderful Counsellor"; & when you have done this, let no importunity of whatever kind prevail over you, & cause you to transgress your own Limitations. I have already exceeded the usual bounds of an Epistle. But you will easily pardon a little prolixity, when I assure you it flows from a heart deeply impressed with a sense of the many difficulties which you must encounter, & the dangers which will surround you when you come first out from the peaceful recess of Contemplation, & enter, young and unexperienced, into the tumultuous undiscerning World. I submit these hints to your consideration, & have nothing more than sincere & ardent wishes for your present & perpetual Felicity.

       I am, Sir,
        yours.
         Philip V. Fithian

To Mr John Peck.
on going to Virginia in
Character of a Tutor.

The economy of the colonial South was one of ever-changing variety. The three major crops—rice, indigo, and tobacco—shared fields with vegetables, grain, and livestock. But the easiest crop to grow in the humid warmth of the tidewater region was tobacco. Since it required the simplest tools and the most accessible skills, tobacco could be grown equally well by the families of small yeomen who were the majority in colonial society or the large planters whose wealth and family records have monopolized our attention. The anonymous American Husbandry *described the cultivation of tobacco for English readers in 1775. The following excerpts are taken from the edition by Harry J. Carmen (New York, 1939), pp. 159-166, 176-177.*

This plant [tobacco] is cultivated in all parts of North America, from Quebec to Carolina, and even the West Indies; but, except in Maryland, Virginia, and North Carolina, they plant no more than for private use, making it an object of such immense consequence.

It was planted in large quantities by the Indians, when we first came to America, and its use from them brought into Europe; but what their method of culture was is now no longer known, as they plant none, but buy what they want of the English. Tobacco is raised from the seed, which is sown in spring upon a bed of rich mould; when about the height of four or five inches, the planter takes the opportunity of rainy weather to transplant them. The ground which is prepared to receive it, is, if it can be got, a rich black mould; fresh woodlands are best: sometimes it is so badly cleared from the stumps of trees, that they cannot give it any ploughings; but in old cultivated lands they plough it several times, and spread on it what manure they can raise. The negroes then hill it; that is, with hoes and shovels they form hillocks, which lie in the manner of Indian corn, only they are larger, and more carefully raked up; the hills are made in squares, from six to nine feet distance, according to the land; the richer it is, the further they are put asunder, as the plants grow higher and spread proportionally. The plants in about a month are a foot high, when they prune and top them; operations, in which they seem to be very wild, and to execute them upon no rational principles; experiments are much wanting on these points, for the planters never go out of the beaten road, but do just as their fathers did, resembling therein the British farmers their brethren. They prune off all the bottom leaves, leaving only seven or eight on a stalk, thinking that such as they leave will be the larger, which is contrary to nature in every instance throughout all vegetation. In six weeks more the tobacco is at its full growth, being then from four and a half to seven feet high: during all this time, the negroes are employed twice a week in pruning off the suckers, clearing the hillocks from weeds, and attending to the worms, which are a great enemy to the plant; when the tobacco changes its colour, turning brown, it is ripe and they then cut it down and lay it close in heaps in the field to sweat one night: the next day they are carried in bunches by the negroes to a building called the tobacco house, where every plant is hung up separate to dry, which takes a month or five weeks; this house excludes the rain, but is designed for the admission of as much air as possible. They are then laid close in heaps in the tobacco houses for a week or a fortnight to sweat again, after which it is sorted and packed up in hogsheads; all the operations after the plants are dried must be done in moist or wet weather, which prevents its crumbling to dust.

There are among many inferior distinctions of sorts, two [of which are] generally attended to, Oroonoko and sweet scented; the latter is of the finest flavour and most valued, growing chiefly in the lower parts of Virginia, viz. on James river and York river, and likewise on the Rappahannock and the south side of the Potomack: the Oroonoko is principally in use on Chesepeak [Chesapeake] bay, and the back settlements on all the rivers. It is strong and hot; the principal markets for it are Germany and the North. . . .

One of the greatest advantages attending the culture of tobacco is the quick, easy, and certain method of sale. This was effected by the inspection law, which took place in Virginia in the year 1730, but not in Maryland until 1748. The planter, by virtue of this, may go to any place and sell his tobacco, without carrying a sample of it along with him, and the merchant may buy it, though lying a hundred miles, or at any distance from his store, and yet be morally sure both with respect to quantity and quality. For this purpose, upon all the rivers and bays of both provinces, at the distance of about twelve or fourteen miles from each other, are erected warehouses, to which all the tobacco in the country must be brought and there lodged, before the planters can offer it to sale; and inspectors are appointed to examine all the tobacco brought in, receive such as is good and merchantable, condemn and burn what appears damnified or insufficient. The greatest part of the tobacco is prized, or put up into hogsheads by the planters themselves, before it is carried to the warehouses. Each hogshead, by an act of assembly, must be 950 lb. neat or upwards; some of them weight 14 cwt. and even 18 cwt. and the heavier they are the merchants like them the better; because four hogsheads, whatsoever their weight be, are esteemed a tun, and pay the same freight. The inspectors give notes of receipt for the tobacco, and the merchants take them in payment for their goods, passing current indeed over the whole colonies; a most admirable invention, which operates so greatly that in Virginia they have no paper currency.

The merchants generally purchase the tobacco in the country, by sending persons to open stores for them; that is, warehouses in which they lay in a great assortment of British commodities and manufactures; to these, as to shops, the planters resort, and supply themselves with what they want, paying, in inspection receipts, or taking on credit according to what will be given them; and as they are in general a very luxurious set of people, they buy too much upon credit; the consequence of which is, their getting in debt to the London merchants, who take mortgages on their plantations, ruinous enough, with the usury of eight per cent. But this is apparently the effect of their imprudence in living upon trust.

Respecting the product of tobacco, they know very little of it themselves by the acre, as they never calculate in that manner, and not many tobacco grounds were ever measured; all their ideas run in proportion per working hand. Some are hired labourers, but in general they are negroe slaves; and the product from the best information I have gained, varies from an hogshead and a half to three and an half per head. The hogshead used to be of the value of 5 £. but of late years it is 8 £. per head, according to the goodness of the lands and other circumstances. But [as for] the planters, none of them depend on tobacco alone, and this is more and more the case since corn has yielded a high price, and since their grounds have begun to be worn out. They all raise corn and provisions enough to support the family plantation, besides exporting considerable quantities; no wheat in the world exceeds in quality that of Virginia and Maryland. Lumber they also send largely to the West Indies. The whole culture of tobacco is over in the summer months; in the winter, the negroes are employed in sawing and butting timber, threshing corn, clearing new land, and preparing for tobacco; so that it is plain, they make a product per head, besides that of tobacco. . . .

There is no plant in the world that requires richer land, or more manure than tobacco; it will grow on poorer fields, but not to yield crops that are sufficiently profitable to pay the expenses of negroes, etc. The land they found to answer best is fresh woodlands, where many ages have formed a stratum of rich black mould. Such land will, after clearing, bear tobacco many years, without any change, prove more profitable to the planter than the power of dung can do on worse lands; this makes the tobacco planters more solicitous for new land than any other people in America, they wanting it much more. Many of them have very handsome houses, gardens, and improvements about them, which fixes them to one spot; but others, when they have exhausted their grounds, will sell them to new settlers for corn-fields, and move backwards with their negroes, cattle, and tools, to take up fresh land for tobacco; this is common, and will continue so as long as good land is to be had upon navigable rivers. . . .

A very considerable tract of land is necessary for a tobacco plantation; first, that the planter may have a sure prospect of increasing his culture on fresh land; secondly, that the lumber may be a winter employment for his slaves and afford casks for his crops. Thirdly, that he may be able to keep vast stocks of cattle for raising provisions in plenty, by ranging in the woods; and where the lands are not fresh, the necessity is yet greater, as they must yield much manure for replenishing the worn-out fields. This want of land is such, that they reckon a planter should have 50 acres of land for every working hand; with less than this they will find themselves distressed for want of room.

But I must observe that great improvements might be made in the culture of this crop; the attention of the planters is to keep their negroes employed on the plants and the small space that the hillocks occupy, being very apt to neglect the intervals; the expence of hoeing them is considerable, and consequently they are apt to be remiss in this work. Here they ought to substitute the horse-hoeing management, which would cost much less, and be an hundred times more effectual. The roots of the tobacco are powerful; they spread far beyond the hillocks, which ought to convince the planters that they should seed them there by good culture, but this is little considered. A few men once got into the use of a plough, invented in the back parts of Virginia, for opening a trench in the intervals, to kill weeds, loosen the earth, and carry the water of hasty rains off; but, from the carelessness of servants, the scheme came to nothing, though it promised better ideas in future. . . .

Before I quit these observations on this part of the husbandry of Virginia and Maryland, I should remark that to make a due profit on tobacco, a man should be able to begin with twenty slaves at least, because so many will pay for an overseer: none, or at least very few, can be kept without an overseer, and if fewer than twenty be the number, the expence of the overseer will be too high; for they are seldom to be gained under £ 25 a year, and generally from 30 to 50 £ . But it does not follow from hence, that settlers are precluded from these colonies who cannot buy twenty negroes; every day's experience tells us the contrary of this; the only difference is, that they begin in small; and either have no slaves at all, or no more than what they will submit to take care of themselves; in this case, they may begin with only one or two, and make a profit proportioned to that of the greater number, without the expence of an overseer. . . .

It is no slight benefit to be able to mix tobacco planting with common husbandry; this is as easily done as can be wished, and is indeed the practice of the greatest planters. A man may be a farmer for corn and provisions, and yet employ a few hands on tobacco, according as his land or manure will allow him. This makes a small business very profitable, and at the same time easy to be attained, nor is any thing more common throughout both Maryland and Virginia.

The population and work force of the colonial South was as varied as its economy. The first settlers were of course Europeans, primarily Englishmen and French Huguenots, who began the intensive agriculture of the tidewater region of Maryland and Virginia and then gradually pushed into the wooded backcountry of the Carolinas. Dr. John Brickell caught the life-styles of the Carolinians for his British readers in The Natural History of North Carolina *(Dublin, 1737), pp. 31-34, 37-38, while Henry Hartwell, James Blair, and Edward Chilton portrayed the better sort of white workers in 1697 in* The Present State of Virginia, and the College *(London, 1727), pp. 6-14.*

The Europians, or Christians of North Carolina, are a streight, tall, well-limb'd and active people; their children being seldom or never troubled with rickets, and many other distempers that the Europians are afflicted with, and you shall seldom see any of them deformed in body.

The men who frequent the woods, and labour out of doors, or use the waters, the vicinity of the sun makes impressions on them; but as for the women that do not expose themselves to weather, they are often very fair, and well featur'd as you shall meet with any where, and have very brisk and charming eyes; and as well and finely shaped, as any women in the world. And I have seldom observ'd any red-hair'd women, or men, born in this country.

They marry generally very young, some at thirteen or fourteen; and she that continues unmarried, until twenty, is reckoned a stale maid, which is a very indifferent character in that country. These marriages for want of an orthodox clergyman, is performed by the governor or the next justice of the peace, who reads the matrimonial ceremony, which is as binding there as if done by the best divine in Europe. The women are very fruitful, most houses being full of little ones, and many women from other places who have been long married and without children, have remov'd to Carolina, and become joyful mothers, as has been often observ'd. It very seldom happens they miscarry, and they have very easie travail in their child-bearing.

The children at nine months old are able to walk and run about the house, and are very docile and apt to learn any thing, as any children in Europe; and those that have the advantage to be educated, write good hands, and prove good accomptants, which is very much coveted and most necessary in these parts. The young men are generally of a bashful, sober behaviour, few proving prodigals, to spend what the parents with care and industry have left them, but commonly improve it.

The girls are most commonly handsome and well featur'd, but have pale or swarthy complexions, and are generally more forward than the boys, notwithstanding the women are very shy, in their discourses, till they are acquainted. The girls are not only bred to the needle and spinning, but to the dairy and domestick affairs, which many of them manage with a great deal of prudence and conduct, though they are very young.

Both sexes are very dexterous in paddling and managing their canoes, both men, women, boys, and girls, being bred to it from their infancy. The women are the most industrious in these parts, and many of them by their good housewifery make a great deal of cloath of their own cotton, wool, and flax, and some of them weave their own cloath with which they decently apparel their whole family though large. Others are so ingenious that they make up all the wearing apparel both for husband, sons and daughters. Others are very ready to help and assist their husbands in any servile work, as planting when the season of the year requires expedition: pride seldom banishing housewifery. Both sexes are most commonly spare of body and not cholerick, nor easily cast down at disappointments and losses, and seldome immoderately grieving at misfortunes in life, excepting it be the loss of their nearest relations.

By the fruitfulness of the women in North Carolina, and the great numbers of men, women, and children, that are daily transported from Europe, they are now become so powerful, in this and most of the other provinces in the hands of the English, that they are able to resist for the future any attempts the Indians may make on them.

Add to this, the several Indian kings that at present are in the Christian interest, who pay some small tribute as an acknowledgement of their subjection, and are ready upon all occasions to assist them when ever they are required to do so; therefore they live at present without any dread or fear of those savages to what they formerly did.

The men are very ingenious in several handy craft businesses, and in building their canoes and houses; though by the richness of the soil, they live for the most part after an indolent and luxurious manner; yet some are laborious, and equalize with the Negro's in hard labour, and others quite the reverse; for I have frequently seen them come to the towns, and there remain drinking rum, punch, and other liquors for eight or ten days successively, and after they have committed this excess, will not drink any spiritous liquor, 'till such time as they take the next Frolick, as they call it, which is generally in two or three months. These excesses are the occasions of many diseases amongst them. But amongst the better sort, or those of good economy, it is quite otherwise, who seldom frequent the taverns, haveing plenty of wine, rum, and other liquors at their own houses, which they generously make use of amongst their friends and acquaintance, after a most decent and discreet manner, and are not so subject to disorders as those who debauch themselves in such a beastly manner. The former sometimes bring their wives with them to be partakers of these Frolicks, which very often is not commendable or decent to behold. . . .

Their houses are built after two different ways; viz. the most substantial planters generally use brick, and lime, which is made from oyster-shell, for there are no stones to be found proper for that purpose but near the mountains; the meaner sort erect with timber, the outside with clap-boards. The roofs of both sorts of houses are made with shingles, and they generally have sash windows, and affect large and decent rooms with good closets, as they do a most beautiful prospect by some noble river or creek.

Their furniture, as with us, consists of pewter, brass, tables, chairs, which are imported here commonly from England: the better sort have tollerable Quantities of plate, with other convenient, ornamental, and valuable furniture.

But now if it be enquir'd what sort of a Country it is after all this, we must represent it after a quite different Manner from what might be expected from the first and eldest of all the English Plantations in

America. As to the outward Appearance, it looks all like a wild Desert; the High-Lands overgrown with Trees, and the Low-Lands sunk with Water, Marsh, and Swamp: the few Plantations and clear'd Grounds bearing no Proportion to the rough and uncultivated.

The Inhabitants are of three Sorts, Planters, Tradesmen, and Merchants.

Tho' the Planters are the most numerous, perhaps not the hundredth Part of the Country is yet clear'd from the Woods, and not one Foot of the Marsh and Swamp drained. As fast as the Ground is worn out with Tobacco and Corn, it runs up again in Underwoods, and in many Places of the Country, that which has been clear'd is thicker in Woods than it was before the clearing. It is but in very few Places that the Plough is made use of, for in their first clearing they never grub up the Stumps, but cut the Trees down about two or three Foot from the Ground; so that all the Roots and Stumps being left, that Ground must be tended with Hoes, and by that time the Stumps are rotten, the Ground is worn out; and having fresh Land enough, of which they must clear some for Fire-Wood, they take but little Care to recruit the old Fields with Dung. Of Grain and Pulse they commonly provide only as much as they expect they themselves shall have Occasion for, for the Use of their Families, there being no Towns or Markets where they can have a ready Vent for them, and scarce any Money to serve for a common Exchange in buying and selling. The only Thing whereof they make as much as they can, is Tobacco, there being always a Vent for that at one Time of the Year or other; besides that their Want of Cloaths and Household-Furniture, and all their other Necessaries, instigate them to make as much Tobacco as they can, this being the Money of that Country which Answers all Things. But the great Labour about Tobacco being only in Summer time, they acquire great Habits of Idleness all the rest of the Year.

For want of Towns, Markets, and Money, there is but little Encouragement for Tradesmen and Artificers, and therefore little Choice of them, and their Labour very dear in the Country. A Tradesman having no Opportunity of a Market where he can buy Meat, Milk, Corn, and all other things, must either make Corn, keep Cows, and raise Stockes himself, or must ride about the Country to buy Meat and Corn where he can find it; and then is puzzled to find Carriers, Drovers, Butchers, Salting, (for he can't buy one Joynt or two) and a great many other Things, which there would be no Occasion for, if there were Towns and Markets. Then a great deal of the Tradesman's Time being necessarilly spent in going and coming to and from his Work, in dispers'd Country Plantations, and his Pay being generally in straggling Parcels of Tobacco, the Collection whereof costs about 10 *per cent.* and the best of this Pay coming but once a Year, so that he cannot turn his Hand frequently with a small Stock, as Tradesmen do in England and elsewhere, all this occasions the Dearth of all Tradesmen's Labour, and likewise the Discouragement, Scarcity, and Insufficiency of Tradesmen.

The Merchants live the best of any in that Country, but yet are subject to great Inconveniencies in the way of their Trade, which might be avoided, if they had Towns, Markets, and Money. For first they are obliged to sell upon Trust all the Year long, except just a little while when Tobacco is ready. 2dly, they likewise drive a pityful retail Trade to serve every Man's little Occasions, being all in Effect but Country Chapmen, for want of Towns to be a Center of Trade and Business. 3dly, Besides the Charge of it, they are necessitated to trust all their Concerns to their Receivers, who go about among the Planters that owe them Tobacco, and receive and mark it for them, which Receivers, if they want either Skill or Honesty, prove very fatal to the Merchant. 4thly, They are at the Charge of carting this Tobacco, so mark'd and receiv'd, to convenient Landings; or if it lyes not far from these Landings, they must trust to the Seamen for their careful rolling it on board of their Sloops and Shallops; and if the Seamen roll it in bad Weather, or dirty Ways, it is expos'd to a great deal of Damage. 5thly, It is a great while before the Ships can be loaded, their Freight lying at such a Distance, and being to be brought together in this scrambling Manner. By Reason of this it is an usual thing with Ships to lye three or four Months in the Country, which might be dispatch'd in a Fortnight's Time, if the Tobacco were ready at certain Ports; and this inhances the Freight to almost double the Price of what it needed to be, if the Ship had a quick Dispatch.

In *New-England* they were oblig'd at their first Settlement to settle in Towns, and would not permit a single Man to take up Land, till a certain Number of Men agreed together, as many as might make a Township; then they laid them out a Town, with Home-Lots for Gardens and Orchards, Out-Lots for Corn-Fields and Meadows, and Country-Lots for Plantations, with Overseers, and Gangs of Hands, which would have prov'd an excellent Way in such a Country as Virginia is. But this Opportunity being lost, they seated themselves, without any Rule or Order in Country Plantations, and being often sensible of the inconveniences of that dispers'd way of living, their General Assemblies have made several Attempts to bring the People into Towns, which have prov'd all ineffectual. One Error has generally run through all these Undertakings, viz. That they always appointed too many Towns, which will be still the Fault of them, if they are contriv'd by a General Assembly; for every Man desiring the Town to be as near as is possible to his own Door, and the Burgesses setting up every one of them for his own County, they have commonly contrived a Town for every County, which might be reasonable enough hereafter, when the Country comes to be well peopled, but at present is utterly impractical for want of People to inhabit them, and Money to build them. And therefore we cannot but think the Governor and Assembly of Mary-Land have taken a much wiser Course, who in their Law for Towns, have order'd only two Towns in that whole Province, viz. one on the eastern, and another on the western Shore. So perhaps two or three Towns in Virginia would be enough at first; the Country might add more afterwards, as they encrease in Wealth and People. Another Error they ran into in their last Law for Towns, was that they made it unlawful to buy or sell any Goods exported or imported, but at these Towns, under no less a Penalty than the Forfeiture of Ship and Goods, which was a great force upon Trade, and would have made all People very uneasy at present; tho' on the other hand there is this to be said for it, that their Merchants being already seated with their Stores in their Country Plantations, and having their Customers all round about them, without some considerable Force could not be induced to leave all these, and to come and live in Towns. Some are of Opinion that the King's constituting Ports for Exportation and Importation would do the Business, i.e. would bring the Trade to these Ports, and perhaps it would be at Long-run; for all that set up for Merchants after such a Constitution of Ports, would probably set up at these Places, but it would at the Long-run; for all that set up for Merchants after such a ent Possession of the Trade, would be perswaded to leave their Country-Houses and Stores, to come and live at Towns. Perhaps if there were great Care taken to encourage these Port-Towns with Privileges and Immunities, and likewise to discourage the Country Stores, the Thing would quickly be more effectual. However it is, *hoc opus, hic labor est*, if Towns and Ports can be brought to bear, the chief Obstruction to the Improvement of that Country will be removed. It is certain that little Help towards it is to be expected from their General Assembly, except they should come to have a Governor in whom they have a most mighty Confidence that he acts for the publick Good; which was the Case in Governor Nicholson's Time, when we see they were not only willing to have Towns, but to force them with many visible Inconveniences. But for their own Temper, they shewed it as soon as he was gone, i.e. they are daily more and more adverse to Cohabitation; the major Part of the House of Burgesses consisting of Virginians that never saw a Town, nor have no Notion of the Conveniency of any other but a Country Life: As a Proof whereof perhaps it may not be unfit to give an Account of an Argument which was brought against Towns by an Ingenious Virginian, who had never been out of the Country: His Argument was this, "That they might observe already, wherever they were thick seated, they could hardly raise any Stocks, or live by one another; much more, concluded he, would it be impossible for us to live, when a matter of an hundred Families are coop'd up within the Compass of half a Mile of Ground.

Besides freemen there were two other groups of workers in the colonial South—servants and apprentices, whose economic freedom was abridged only for a specified time, and perpetual slaves. The following documents describe the social, economic, and legal condition of these groups. The first is the view of one of Virginia's wealthy planters, Robert Beverley (1673-1722). It is taken from his History and Present State of Virginia *(London, 1705), edited by David Freeman Hawke (Indianapolis, 1971), pp. 140-142.*

Their servants they distinguish by the names of slaves for life and servants for a time.

Slaves are the Negroes and their posterity following the condition of the mother, according to the maxim *partus sequitur ventrem*. They are called slaves in respect of the time of their servitude because it is for life.

Servants are those which serve only for a few years, according to the time of their indenture or the custom of the country. The custom of the country takes place upon such as have no indentures. The law in this case is that if such servants be under nineteen years of age, they must be brought into court to have their age adjudged, and from the age they are judged to be of they must serve until they reach four and twenty. But if they be adjudged upwards of nineteen, they are then only to be servants for the term of five years.

The male servants and slaves of both sexes are employed together in tilling and manuring the ground, in sowing and planting tobacco, corn, etc. Some distinction, indeed, is made between them in their clothes and food, but the work of both is no other than what the overseers, the freemen, and the planters themselves do.

Sufficient distinction is also made between the female servants and slaves, for a white woman is rarely or never put to work in the ground if she be good for anything else. And to discourage all planters from using any women so, their law imposes the heaviest taxes upon female servants working in the ground, while it suffers all other white women to be absolutely exempted. Whereas on the other hand, it is a common thing to work a woman slave out of doors; nor does the law make any distinction in her taxes, whether her work be abroad or at home.

Because I have heard how strangely cruel and severe the service of this country is represented in some parts of England, I can't forbear affirming that the work of their servants and slaves is no other than what every common freeman does. Neither is any servant required to do more in a day than his overseer. And I can assure you with a great deal of truth that generally their slaves are not worked near so hard nor so many hours in a day as the husbandmen and day laborers in England. An overseer is a man that having served his time has acquired the skill and character of an experienced planter and is therefore entrusted with the direction of the servants and slaves.

But to complete this account of servants I shall give you a short relation of the care their laws take that they be used as tenderly as possible.

BY THE LAWS OF THEIR COUNTRY

1. All servants whatsoever have their complaints heard without fee or reward, but if the master be found faulty the charge of the complaint is cast upon him, otherwise the business is done *ex officio*.

2. Any justice of peace may receive the complaint of a servant and order everything relating thereto till the next county court, where it will be finally determined.

3. All masters are under the correction and censure of the county

courts to provide for their servants good and wholesome diet, clothing, and lodging.

4. They are always to appear upon the first notice given of the complaint of their servants, otherwise to forfeit the service of them until they do appear.

5. All servants' complaints are to be received at any time in court without process and shall not be delayed for want of form. But the merits of the complaint must be immediately inquired into by the justices, and if the master cause any delay therein the court may remove such servants if they see cause until the master will come to trial.

6. If a master shall at any time disobey an order of court made upon any complaint of a servant, the court is empowered to remove such servant forthwith to another master who will be kinder, giving to the former master the produce only (after fees deducted) of what such servants shall be sold for by public outcry.

7. If a master should be so cruel as to use his servant ill that is fallen sick or lame in his service and thereby rendered unfit for labor, he must be removed by the church wardens out of the way of such cruelty and boarded in some good planter's house till the time of his freedom, the charge of which must be laid before the next county court, which has power to levy the same from time to time upon the goods and chattels of the master. After which the charge of such boarding is to come upon the parish in general.

8. All hired servants are entitled to these privileges.

9. No master of a servant can make a new bargain for service or other matter with his servant without the privity and consent of a justice of peace, to prevent the master's overreaching or scaring such servant into an unreasonable compliance.

10. The property of all money and goods sent over thither to servants, or carried in with them, is reserved to themselves and remain entirely at their disposal.

11. Each servant at his freedom receives of his master fifteen bushels of corn (which is sufficient for a whole year) and two new suits of clothes, both linen and woolen, and then becomes as free in all respects and as much entitled to the liberties and privileges of the country as any other of the inhabitants or natives are.

12. Each servant has then also a right to take up fifty acres of land, where he can find any unpatented; but that is no great privilege, for anyone may have as good a right for a piece of eight.

This is what the laws prescribe in favor of servants, by which you may find that the cruelties and severities imputed to that country are an unjust reflection. For no people more abhor the thoughts of such usage than the Virginians, nor take more precaution to prevent it.

After the introduction of Negro slaves in 1619 the balance between white and black servants eventually became a concern to the leaders of the southern colonies. As the rice culture of South Carolina drew more and more slaves after 1690, the legislature sought to encourage the importation of white servants to maintain a numerical balance. The act which they passed in 1698 is taken from Thomas Cooper, ed. Statutes at Large of South Carolina *(Columbia, 1836-41), vol. 2, pp. 153-156.*

Whereas, the great number of negroes which of late have been imported into this Collony may endanger the safety thereof if speedy care be not taken and encouragement given for the importation of white servants.

I. Be it enacted by his Excellency, John Earl of Bath, Palatine, and the rest of the true and absolute Lords and Proprietors of the Province, by and with the advice and consent of the rest of the members of the Generall Assembly now met at Charlestowne, for the south-west part of this Province, that every merchant, owner or master of any ship or vessel, or any other person not intending to settle and plant here, which shall bring any white male servants, Irish only excepted, into Ashley River, above sixteen years of age and under forty, and the same shall deliver to the Receiver General, shall receive and be paid by the said Receiver in dollars or pieces of eight, at five shillings the piece, the sum of thirteen pounds for every servant so delivered, and for every boy of twelve years and under sixteen, imported and delivered to the Receiver as aforesaid, the sum of twelve pounds, as aforesaid; Provided that every servant, as aforesaid, hath not less than four years to serve from and after the day of his arrival in Ashley River, and every boy aforesaid, not less than seven years. . . .

II. And be it further enacted by the authority aforesaid, that no servant or boy shall serve longer than such time they have indented and contracted for, and that every servant above sixteen years old which shall be brought into Ashley River without contract or indenture, shall serve five years and no longer; and every boy from twelve years old to fourteen shall serve till they come to one and twenty years old, and from fourteen years old to sixteen years shall serve seven years and no longer.

III. And be it further enacted, that every owner of every plantation to which doth belong six men negro slaves above sixteen years old, shall take from the Receiver one servant, when it shall happen to be his lot to have one, and shall within three months pay the said Receiver so much money for the said servant as the Receiver gave to the 1/2 person from whom he received the same; and the owner of every plantation to which doth belong twelve negro men, as aforesaid, shall when it shall be his lot, take two servants as aforesaid; and every master of every plantation proportionably; Provided, and it is hereby intended, that every male servant contracted for four years, and not under, shall to all intents and purposes be deemed as good, and supply the room of such as shall be bought from on board of any vessel, or by lot should be appointed him as aforesaid.

IV. And that no master of any plantation may have any servant put unduly and unjustly upon him, but the same it shall be his lot to have, and not till it shall be his lot thereto,

Be it enacted, that every constable, in his division, under the penalty of forty shillings, shall make a lyst of the names of all masters of plantations, to whom six negro men or upwards do belong, and the same shall deliver to the publick Receiver for the time being [and servants shall be assigned to plantations by lots drawn from these lists. Servants shall be allotted first to all plantations with twelve Negroes or more and then to plantations with six negros, until the provisions of Section III shall be met.]

Read three times, and ratified in open Assembly, the 8th day
of October, 1698.

In an economy that demanded high concentrations of labor, the relations between master and servant required the minute regulation of the civil government. The North Carolina act of 1741, which ran to 58 sections, is drawn from the State Records of North Carolina *(Goldsboro, 1886-1907), ed. Walter Clark vol. 23, pp. 191-204. The Virginia statutes concerning apprenticeship are taken from William*

W. Hening, The Statutes at Large; Being a Collection of All the Laws of Virginia . . . (Richmond, Philadelphia, 1819-1823), vol. 1, pp. 336-337; vol. 3, pp. 375-376; vol. 8, pp. 374-377.

I. Be it Enacted, by his Excellency Gabriel Johnston, Esq., Governor, by and with the advice and consent of his Majesty's Council, and General Assembly of this Province, and it is hereby enacted, by the authority of the same, that no person whatsoever, being a Christian, or of Christian parentage, who, from and after the ratification of this act, shall be imported or brought into this province, shall be deemed a servant for any term of years, unless the person importing him or her shall produce an indenture, or some specialty or agreement, signifying that the person so imported did contract to serve such importer, or his assigns, any number of years, in consideration of his or her passage, or some other consideration of his or her therein expressed: and upon any contest arising between the master of any vessel, or other person importing any servant or servants, without indenture, upon any bargain or specialty as aforesaid, the same shall be determined at the next county court to be held for the county where the said servant or servants shall be imported, the justices of which court are hereby impowered to hear and determine the same, in a summary way: and such determination or judgment shall be conclusive and binding on the importer of servant or servants, either for the discharge of the said servant or servants, or to oblige him, her, or them, to serve the importer, or his assigns, as the matter shall appear.

II. And be it further enacted, by the authority aforesaid, that if any christian servant, whether he or she be a servant by importation or otherwise, shall at any time or times absent him or herself from the service of his or her master or mistress, without licence first had, he or she shall satisfy and make good such loss of time by serving after their time of service by indenture or otherwise is expired, double the time of service lost or neglected by such absence: and also such longer time as the county court shall think fit to adjudge, in consideration of any further charge or damage the master or mistress of such servant may have sustained, by reason of his or her absence as aforesaid.

III. And be it further enacted, by the authority aforesaid, that if any christian servant shall lay violent hands on his or her master or mistress, or overseer, or shall obstinately refuse to obey the lawful commands of any of them, upon proof thereof by one or more evidences before any justice of the peace, he or she shall, for every such offence, suffer such corporal punishment the said judge shall think fit to adjudge, not exceeding twenty-one lashes.

IV. And as an encouragement for christian servants to perform their service with fidelity and cheerfulness; be it further enacted, by the authority aforesaid, that all masters and owners of any servant or servants shall find and provide for their servant or servants wholesome and competent diet, clothing and the lodging, at the discretion of the county court, and shall not, at any time, give immoderate correction, neither shall at any time whip a christian servant naked, without an order from the justice of the peace. And if any person shall presume to whip a christian servant naked, without such order, the person so offending shall forfeit and pay the sum of forty shillings, proclamation money, to the party injured; to be recovered, with costs, upon petition to the county court (without the formal process of an action), as in and by this act is provided for servants' complaints to be heard and determined: provided complaint be made six months after such whipping. . . .

XVII. And whereas many women servants are begotten with child by free men, or servants, to the great prejudice of their master or mistress, whom they serve, be it therefore enacted, by the authority aforesaid, that if any women servant shall hereafter be with child, and bring forth the same during the time of her servitude, she shall for such offence be adjusted by the county court to serve her master or mistress one year after her term of service by indenture or otherwise is expired.

XVIII. And be it further enacted, by the authority aforesaid, that if any woman servant shall hereafter be delivered of a child, begotten by her master, such servant shall immediately after delivery be sold by the church wardens of the parish. And if any white servant woman shall, during the time of her servitude, be delivered of a child begotten by any Negro, mulatto, or Indian, such servant, over and above the time she is by this act to serve her master or owner for such offence, shall be sold by the church wardens of the parish, for two years, after the time by indenture or otherwise is expired: and the money arising thereby applied to the use of the said parish; and such mulatto child or children of such servant, to be bound by the county court until he or she arrives at the age of thirty-one years. . . .

XXXIX. And be it further enacted, by the authority aforesaid, that if any negro or other person, who shall be taken up as a runaway and brought before any justice of the peace, and cannot speak English, or through obstinacy, will not declare the name of his or her owner, such justice shall in such case, and he is hereby required, by a warrant under his hand, to commit the said negro, slave, or runaway to the gaol of the county wherein he or she shall be taken up: and the sheriff or under-sheriff of the county into whose custody the said runaway shall be committed, shall forthwith cause notice, in writing, of such commitment to be set up on the court-house door of the said county, and there continued during the space of two months; in which notice a full description of the said runaway and his clothing shall be particularly set down: and shall cause a copy of such notice to be sent to the clerk or reader of each church or chappel within his county, who are hereby required to make publication thereof, by setting up the same in some open and convenient place, near the said church or chappel, on every Lord's Day for the space of two months from the date thereof. And every sheriff failing to give such notice as is herein directed shall forfeit and pay five pounds, proclamation money; which said forfeiture shall and may be recovered with costs in any court of record in this government by action of debt, bill, plaint, or information, wherein no essoign, privilege, protection, injunction or wager of law shall be allowed. The one moiety whereof shall be to the church wardens, for the use of the parish, as well as towards the defraying of the charges that shall arise and become due by virtue of this act, and the other moiety to the person who shall sue for the same. . . .

XLIV. And be it further enacted, by the authority aforesaid, that no slave shall be permitted, on any pretence whatsoever, to raise any horses, cattle or hogs; and all horses, cattle and hogs that six months from the date thereof, shall belong to any slave or of any slave's mark in this government, shall be seized and sold by the church wardens of the parish where such horses, cattle or hogs shall be, and the profit thereof be applied, one half to the use of the said parish, and the other half to the informer.

XLV. And whereas many times slaves run away and lie out hid and lurking in the swamps, woods, and other obscure places, killing cattle and hogs, and committing other injuries to the inhabitants in this government: Be it therefore enacted, by the authority aforesaid, that in all such cases, upon intelligence of any slave or slaves lying out as aforesaid, any two justices of the peace for the county wherein such slave or slaves is or are supposed to lurk to do mischief, shall, and they are hereby impowered and required, to issue proclamation against such slave or slaves (reciting his or their name or names, and the name or names of the owner or owners, if known), thereby requiring him or them, and every of them, forthwith to surrender him or themselves: and also, to impower and require the sheriff of the said county to take such power with him as he shall think fit and necessary for going in search and pursuit of and effectual apprehending such outlying slave or slaves; which proclamation shall be published on a Sabbath Day, at the door of every church or chappel or for want of such, at the place where divine service shall be performed in the said county, by the parish clerk or reader, immediately after divine service: And if any slave or slaves against whom proclamation hath been thus issued, stay out and do not immediately return home, it shall be lawful for any person or persons whatsoever to kill and destroy such slave or slaves by such ways and means as he or she shall think fit, without accusation or impeachment of any crime for the same.

1642

Whereas sundry laws and statutes by act of parliament established, have with great wisdome ordained, for the better educateing of youth in honest and profitable trades and manufactures, as also to avoyd sloath and idlenesse wherewith such young children are easily corrupted, as also for releife of such parents whose poverty extends not to give them breeding. That the justices of the peace should at their discretion, bind out children to tradesmen or husbandmen to be brought up in some good and lawfull calling, And whereas God Almighty, among many his other blessings, hath vouchsafed increase of children to this collony, who now are multiplied to a considerable number, who if instructed in good and lawfull trades may much improve the honor and reputation of the country, and noe lesse their owne good and theire parents comfort: But forasmuch as for the most part the parents, either through fond indulgence or perverse obstinacy, are most averse and unwilling to parte with theire children, *Be it therefore inacted by authoritie of this Grand Assembly*, according to the aforesayd laudable custom in the kingdom of England, That the comissioners of the severall countyes respectively do, at theire discretion, make choice of two children in each county of the age of eight or seaven years at the least, either male or female, which are to be sent up to James Citty between this and June next to be imployed in the public flax houses under such master and mistresse as shall be there appointed, In carding, knitting and spinning, &c. And that the said children be furnished from the said county with sixe barrells of corne, two coverletts, or one rugg and one blankett: One bed, one wooden bowle or tray, two pewter spoones, a sow shote of sixe months old, two laying hens, with convenient apparell both linen and woollen, with hose and shooes, And for the better provision of howseing for the said children, *It is inacted*, That there be two houses built by the first of April next of forty foot long a peece with good and substantial timber, The houses to be twenty foot broad apeece, eight foot high in the pitche and a stack of brick chimneys standing in the midst of each house, and that they be lofted with sawne boardes and made with convenient partitions, And it is further thought fitt that the commissioners have caution not to take up any children but from such parents who by reason of their poverty are disabled to maintaine and educate them, *Be it likewise agreed*, That the Governour hath agreed with the Assembly for the sume of 10000 lb. of tob'o. to be paid him the next crop, to build and finish the said howses in manner and form before expressed.

1705

And be it further enacted, That every county court shall take good security of all guardians, for the estates of the orphans committed to their charge, and that they shall yearly inquire into such securities; and if any of them become defective or insufficient, shall cause new security to be given: And if it shall appear that the said estates are likely to be imbezzelled, or that the orphans are not taken care of, and educated according to their estates; then the said court shall have power to remove the said orphans (not being of age to choose their guardians) and their estates, and to place them under the care of such other persons, as to them shall seem most proper; always taking good security for the said orphans estates, that when the same shall become paiable to the said orphans, they shall be paid without making any abatement or allowance (other than of the profits of the said estates) for diet, cloathing, or any other matter whatsoever: And if the estate of any orphan be of so small a value, that no person will maintain him for the profits thereof, then such orphan shall, by direction of the court, be bound apprentice to some handicraft trade, or mariner, until he shall attain to the age of one and twenty years. And the master of every such orphan shall be obliged to teach him to read and write: And, at the expiration of his servitude, to pay and allow him in like manner as is appointed for servants, by indenture or custom. And if it shall appear, that any such apprentice be ill used by his master, or that he fails to teach him his trade, the court shall have power to remove him, and to bind him to such other person as to them shall seem most proper.

1769

WHEREAS the laws now in force are not sufficient to provide for the security and indemnifying the parishes from the great charges frequently arising from children begotten and born out of lawful matrimony: For remedy whereof, *Be it enacted, by the Governor, Council, and Burgesses, of this present General Assembly, and it is hereby enacted by the authority of the same*, That, from and after the passing this act, if any single woman, not being a servant or slave, shall be delivered of a bastard child which shall be chargeable, or likely to become chargeable, to any parish, and shall, upon examination to be taken in writing, upon oath, before any justice of the peace of the county wherein such parish shall lie, charge any person, not being a servant, with being the father of such bastard child, it shall and may be lawful for any justice of the peace of the county wherein the person so charged shall be a resident or inhabitant, upon application made to him by the church-wardens of the parish wherein such child shall be born, or by any one of them, to issue his warrant for the immediate apprehending the persons so charged as aforesaid, and for bringing him before such justice, or before any other justice of the peace of the county wherein he is a resident or inhabitant; and the justice before whom such person shall be brought is hereby authorized and required to commit the person so charged as aforesaid to the common gaol of his county, unless he shall enter into a recognizance, with sufficient security, in the sum of ten pounds, upon condition to appear at the next court to be held for such county, and to abide by and perform such order or orders as shall be made by the said court; and if, upon the circumstances of the case, such court shall adjudge the person so charged to be the father of such bastard child, and that such child is likely to become chargeable to the parish, they shall, and may, by their discretion, take order for keeping such bastard child, by charging the father with the payment of money or tobacco for the maintenance of such child, in such manner, and in such proportions, as they shall think meet and convenient, and for such time as such child is likely to become chargeable to the parish, and no longer. And the father of such child shall enter into a recognizance, with sufficient securities, before the said court, in such sum as the said court, in their discretion, shall think fit, payable to his majesty, his heirs and successors, to observe and perform such order or orders of the court as aforesaid. And if the father, charged with the maintenance of such bastard child as aforesaid, shall make default, and not pay the money or tobacco so as aforesaid charged upon him by order of the said court, to the churchwardens of the parish, for the maintenance of such child, the court before whom such recognizance was entered into, shall, from time to time, upon the motion of the churchwardens of the said parish, or any one of them, enter up judgment and award execution for the money or tobacco in such order or orders mentioned, as the same shall become due, against the said father and his securities, their executors or administrators; provided ten days notice be given to the parties against whom such motion is made, before the making thereof. And if the father of such child shall refuse to enter into recognizance as aforesaid, such father shall be committed by the said court to the common gaol of the county, there to remain, without bail or mainprize, until he shall enter into such recognizance as aforesaid, or until he shall discharge himself by taking the oath of an insolvent debtor, and delivering in a schedule of his estate in manner directed, by the laws now in force, for debtors in execution (and which estate shall, by order of the court, be applied towards indemnifying the parish as aforesaid) or until the churchwardens of the parish concerned shall otherwise consent to his discharge.

II. *Provided always*, That it shall not be lawful for any justice, or justices of the peace, to send for any woman whatsoever, before she shall be delivered, in order to her being examined concerning her pregnancy, or compel her to answer any questions relating thereto, before her delivery.

III. *And be it further enacted, by the authority aforesaid*, That if any single woman, not being a servant, shall be delivered of a bastard child, she shall be liable to pay the sum of twenty shillings, current money of Virginia, to the churchwardens of the parish wherein she shall be delivered; to be recovered, with costs, before a justice of peace, and on such judgment execution may issue as in other cases: But the person so convicted shall not be liable to be shipped for failing to make payments, or to give security for such fine, any law to the contrary notwithstanding; which fine, recovered as aforesaid, shall be applied by the churchwardens to the use of the poor of the parish.

IV. *And be it further enacted, by the authority aforesaid*, That every such bastard child shall be bound apprentice by the churchwardens of the parish, for the time being, wherein such child shall be born, every male until he shall attain the age of twenty-one years, and every female until she shall attain the age of eighteen years, and no longer; and the master or mistress of every such apprentice shall find and provide for him or her diet, cloaths, lodging, and accommodations fit and necessary, and shall teach, or cause him or her to be taught to read and write, and at the expiration of his or her apprenticeship, shall pay every such apprentice the like allowance as is by law appointed for servants, by indenture or custom, and on refusal, shall be compellable thereto in like manner. And if, upon complaint made to the county court, it shall appear that any such apprentice is ill used, or not taught the trade or profession to which he or she may be bound, it shall be lawful for such court to remove and bind him or her to such other person or persons as they shall think fit.

V. And whereas by an act of assembly made in the twenty-seventh year of the reign of King George the second, intituled An act for the better government of servants and slaves, it is amongst other things enacted, if any woman servant shall be delivered of a bastard child, within the time of her service, that, in recompense for the loss and trouble occasioned her master or mistress thereby, she shall, for every such offence, serve her said master or owner one whole year, after her time, by indenture, custom, or former order of courts, shall be expired, or pay her master or owner one thousand pounds of tobacco; and the reputed father, if free, shall give security to the churchwardens of the parish to maintain the child, and keep the parish indemnified, or be compelled thereto, by order of the county court, upon the complaint of the churchwardens. And whereas it frequently happens that convict servants are delivered of such bastard children, who, being disabled to give testimony, cannot be examined, nor for that reason can the reputed father of such bastard child be discovered, and the parish indemnified from the charge of its maintainance: For remedy whereof,

VI. *Be it enacted*, That where any convict servant woman shall be delivered of a bastard child, during the time of her service, the master or owner of such servant shall be obliged to maintain such child, or be compelled thereto by the county court, on complaint of the churchwardens, and, in consideration of such maintainance, shall be intitled to the service of such child, if a male until he shall arrive to the age of twenty-one years, if a female until she shall arrive to the age of eighteen years.

VII. *Provided always*, That such master or owner shall find and provide for such child, the like accommodations, education, and freedom dues, and shall be compelled to answer his or her complaint, made to the county court, for default therein, or for ill usage, in like manner; as is before directed in the case of other apprentices.

At the bottom of the economic and social scale were the Negro slaves. Dr. John Brickell described those of North Carolina in The Natural History of North Carolina *(Dublin, 1737), pp. 272-275, and Hugh Jones, a Virginia minister and professor at the College of William and Mary, those of his own colony in* The Present State of Virginia *[1724], edited by Richard L. Morton (Chapel Hill, 1956), pp. 75-76.*

The Negroes are sold on the coast of Guinea, to merchants trading to those parts, are brought from thence to Carolina, Virginia, and other provinces in the hands of the English, are daily increasing in this country, and generally afford a good price, viz. more or less according to their goodness and age, and are always sure commodities for gold or silver, most other things being purchased with their paper money. Some of them are sold at sixteen, twenty five, or twenty six pounds sterling each, and are looked upon as the greatest riches in these parts. There are great numbers of them born here, which prove more industrious, honest, and better slaves than any brought from Guinea; this is particularly owing to their education amongst the Christians, which very much polishes and refines them from their barbarous and stubborn natures that they are most commonly endued with. I have frequently seen them whipt to that degree, that large pieces of their skin have been hanging down their backs; yet I never observed one of them shed a tear, which plainly shows them to be a people of very harsh and stubborn dispositions.

There are several laws made against them in this province to keep them in subjection, and particularly one, viz, that if a Negroe cut or wound his master or a christian with any unlawful weapon, such as a sword, scymiter, or even a knife, and there is blood-shed, if it is known amongst the planters, they immediately meet and order him to be hanged, which is always performed by another Negroe, and generally the planters bring most of their Negroes with them to behold their fellow Negroe suffer, to deter them from the like vile practice. This law may seem to be too harsh amongst us, to put a man to death for blood-shed only, yet if the severest laws were not strictly put in execution against these people, they would soon overcome the christians in this and most of the other provinces in the hands of the English.

Notwithstanding the many severe laws in force against them, yet they sometimes rise and rebel against their masters and planters, and do a great deal of mischief, being both treacherous and cruel in their natures, so that mild laws would be of no use against them when any favourable opportunity offered of executing their barbarities upon the Christians, as hath been too well experienced in Virginia, and other places, where they have rebelled and destroyed many families.

When they have been guilty of these barbarous and disobedient proceedings, they generally fly to the woods, but as soon as the Indians have notice from the Christians of their being there, they disperse them; killing some, others flying for mercy to the Christians (whom they have injured) rather than fall into the others hands, who have a natural aversion to the Blacks, and put them to death with most exquisite tortures they can invent, whenever they catch them.

When any of these Negroes are put to death by the laws or the country, the planters suffer little or nothing by it, for the province is obliged to pay the full value they judge them worth to the owner; this is the common custom of law in this province, to prevent the planters being ruined by the loss of their slaves, whom they have purchased at so dear a rate; neither is this too burthensom, for I never knew but one put to death here for wounding, and after attempting to kill his master, who used all means he could to save his Life, but to no purpose, for the country insisted on having the law put into execution against him.

The Negroes that most commonly rebel, are those brought from Guinea, who have been inured to war and hardship all their lives; few born here, or in the other provinces have been guilty of these vile practises, except over-persuaded by the former, whose designs they have sometimes discovered to the Christians; some of whom have been rewarded with their freedom for their good services; but the reader must observe, that they are not allowed to be witnesses in any cases whatever, only against one another.

There are some Christians so charitable as to have the Negroes born in the country, baptized and instructed in the Christian Faith in their infancy, which gives them an abhorance of the temper and practice of those who are brought from Guinea. This freedom does not in the least exempt them from their master's servitude, whatever others may imagine to the contrary, who believe them to be at their own liberty as soon as they have received baptism. The planters call these Negroes thus baptized, by any whimsical name their fancy suggests, as Jupiter, Mars, Venus, Diana, Strawberry, Violet, Drunkard, Readdy Money, Piper, Fidler, etc.

Their marriages are generally performed amongst themselves, there being very little ceremony used upon that head; for the man makes the woman a present, such as a brass ring or some other toy, which if she accepts of, becomes his wife; but if ever they part from each other, which frequently happens, upon any little disgust, she returns his present these kind of contracts no longer binding them, than the woman keeps the pledge given her. It frequently happens, when these women have no children by the first husband, after being a year or two cohabiting together, the planters oblige them to take a second, third, fourth, fifth, or more husbands or bedfellows; a fruitful woman amongst them being very much valued by the planters, and a numerous issue esteemed the greatest riches in this country. The children all go with the mother, and are the property of the planter to whom she belongs. And though they have no other ceremony in their Marriages than I have represented, yet they seem to be jealously inclined, and fight most desperately amongst themselves when they rival each other, which they commonly do.

Their children are carefully brought up, and provided for by the planters, 'till they are able to work in the plantations, where they have convenient houses built for them, and they are allowed to plant a sufficient quantity of tobacco for their own use, a part of which they sell, and likewise on Sundays, they gather snake-root, otherwise it would be excessive dear if the Christians were to gather it; with this and the tobacco they buy hats, and other necessaries for themselves, as Linnen, Bracelets, Ribbons, and several other toys for their wives and mistresses.

There are abundance of them given to theft, and frequently steal from each other, and sometimes from the Christians, especially rum, with which they entertain their wives and mistresses at night, but are often detected and punished for it.

The Negroes [of Virginia] live in small cottages called quarters, in about six in a gang, under the direction of an overseer or bailiff; who takes care that they tend such land as the owner allots and orders, upon which they raise hogs and cattle, and plant Indian corn (or maize) and tobacco for the use of their master; out of which the overseer has a dividend (or share) in proportion to the number of hands including himself; this with several privileges is his salary, and is an ample recompence for his pains, and encouragement of his industrious care, as to the labour, health, and provision of the Negroes.

The Negroes are very numerous, some gentlemen having hundreds of them of all sorts, to whom they bring great profit; for the sake of which they are obliged to keep them well, and not overwork, starve, or famish them, besides other inducements to favour them; which is done in a great degree, to such especially that are laborious, careful, and honest; though indeed some masters, careless of their own interest or reputation, are too cruel and negligent.

The Negroes are not only encreased by fresh supplies from Africa and the West India Islands, but also are very prolifick among themselves; and they that are born there talk good English, and affect our language, habits, and customs; and though they be naturally of a barbarous and cruel temper, yet are they kept under by severe discipline upon occasion, and by good laws are prevented from running away, injuring the English, or neglecting their business.

Their work (or chimerical hard slavery) is not very laborious; their greatest hardship consisting in that they and their posterity are not at their own liberty or disposal, but are the property of their owners; and when they are free, they know not how to provide so well for themselves generally; neither did they live so plentifully nor (many of them) so easily in their own country, where they are made slaves to one another, or taken captive by their enemies.

The children belong to the master of the woman that bears them; and such as are born of a Negroe and an European are called Molattoes; but such as are born of an Indian and Negroe are called Mustees.

Their work is to take care of the stock, and plant corn, tobacco, fruits, etc. which is not harder than thrashing, hedging, or ditching; besides, though they are out in the violent heat, wherein they delight, yet in wet or cold weather there is little occasion for their working in the fields, in which few will let them be abroad, lest by this means they might get sick or die, which would prove a great loss to their owners, a good Negroe being sometimes worth three (nay four) score pounds sterling, if he be a tradesman; so that upon this (if upon no other account) they are obliged not to overwork them, but to cloath and feed them sufficiently, and take care of their health.

Several of them are taught to be sawyers, carpenters, smiths, coopers, etc. and though for the most part they be none of the aptest or nicest; yet they are by nature cut out for hard labour and fatigue, and will perform tolerably well; though they fall much short of an Indian, that has learned and seen the same things; and those Negroes make the best servants, that have been slaves in their own country; for they that have been kings and great men there are generally lazy, haughty, and obstinate; whereas the others are sharper, better humoured, and more laborious.

The languages of the new Negroes are various harsh jargons, and their religions and customs such as are best described by Mr. Bosman in his book intitled (I think) *A Description of the Coasts of Africa*.

The nature of the work performed by servants is further revealed by the following documents. The first, a list of indented passengers bound for Virginia, is taken from The Journal of John Harrower, *edited by Edward Miles Riley (Williamsburg, 1963), pp. 166-168. The second is a letter of instructions from a large planter, Richard Corbin, Esq., to his agent, James Semple, for the management of his plantations in Virginia. It is taken from Ulrich B. Phillips, ed.,* Documentary History of American Industrial Society *(Cleveland, 1910), vol. 1, pp. 109-112.*

An account of all Persons who have taken their passage on Board any Ship or Vessel, to go out of this Kingdom from any Port in

England with a description of their Age, Quality, Occupation or Employment. former residence, to what port or place they propose to go, & on what Account, & for what purposes they leave the Country. from the *7th* to the *13th* February 1774. distinguishing each Port.

EMBARKED from the PORT OF LONDON.

Names	Age	Quality, Occupation, or Employment.	Former Residence
Francis Simpson	22	Glass Blower	Surry
John Broomfield	36	Stocking Weaver	Hereford
George Wild	21	Groom	York
Benjamin Badger	22	Husbandman	Do.
William Payne	21	Clerk & Bookkeeper	London
James Sutherland	18	Cordwainer	Do
Edwd. Fitzpatrick	31	Surgeon	Do
George Adams	25	Husbandman	Derby
Willm. Coventry	27	Ropemaker	Southwark
John Connery	40	Perukemaker	Do.
Alexr. Burnett	25	Clerk & Bookkeeper	Westminster
John Tran	20	Carpenter & Joiner	Southwark
James Packer	20	Founder	London
Edwd. Dougharty	20	Gardner	Do
George Boorer	24	Clerk & Bookkeeper	Do
Frederick Pampe	22	Watch & Clockmaker	Do
Mark Mitchell	19	Perukemaker	Do
James Owen	21	Bricklayer	Do
Robert Cowdell	17	Stocking Weaver	Leicester
Law Bagnall	28	Bucklemaker	Birmingham
John Turner	27	Cordwainer	London
John Kennelly	21	Bricklayer	Do
William Dunn	36	Do	Durham
Roger Nichols	40	Breeches Maker	Wilts
Joseph Ormond	24	Hatt Maker	Middlesex
Thomas Rand	22	Butcher	Ireland
William Sibery	47	Weaver	London

Peter Cooley	38	Do	Do
Peter Cooley junr.	18	Do	Do
John Cooley	16	Do	Do
Joseph Cooley	12	Do	Do
Robert Innis	23	Groom	Bristol
Benjamin Ogle	23	Pipemaker	Newcastle
James Freeman	20	Blacksmith	Northampton
Benjamin Thompson	27	Clock & Watchmaker	London
Richard Harris	29	Husbandman	Worcester
Daniel Lakenan	22	Cabinet maker	London
William Wood	29	Husbandman	Northampton
John Harrower	40	Clerk & Bookkeeper	Shetland
Thomas Ford	32	Carver & Gilder	London
John Williams	27	Husbandman	Do
Joseph Clark	21	Cordwainer	Do
Charles Avery	38	White Smith	Do
Thomas Richards	22	Perukemaker	Do
Edward Lawrance	41	Gardner	Middlesex
Thomas Low	17	Cabinet Maker	Chester
Mathew Fright	33	Husbandman	Kent
Peter Collins	40	Cordwainer	London
Alexander Kenneday	38	Cooper	Southwark
John Burton	22	Bricklayer	Ireland
Henry Newland	22	Silk Weaver	London
Thomas Rackstrow	38	Taylor	Do
James Nowland	38	Bricklayer	Do
Alexander Steward	21	Footman	Do
Charles Leslie	37	Tayler	Do
William Bradley	34	Tilemaker & Burner	London
Peter Woillidge	24	Painter & Glazier	Suffolk
William Phillips	41	Baker	London
John Sanders	15	Husbandman	Essex
Jeremiah Stacey	19	Linen Weaver	London
Richard Green	35	Farmer	Lincoln
Daniel Turner	22	Groom	London
John Bateman	23	Clerk & Bookkeeper	Westmoreland
John Goldin	25	Weaver	Wilts
Roger Wren	17	Cooper	London

James Downes	29	Husbandman	Do
John Mitchel	23	Smith & Farrier	Bristol
Thomas Davis	40	Husbandman	London
Henry Featson	22	Bricklayer	Southwark
John Powell	36	Boat Builder	Do
William Hudson	20	Linen Weaver	London
Samuel Mitchel	24	Cooper	York
Thomas Progers	23	Cordwainer	London
William Salton	42	Gardener	Middlesex
Harman Hester	44	Do.	London

75 to Virginia

to what port or place Bound-Virginia
by what Ship-Planter
Masters Name-Daniel Bowers.
for what purpose they leave the Country—Indented Servants for Four Years.

January 1, 1759

MR. JAMES SEMPLE:

As it will be necessary to say something to you and to suggest to you my thoughts upon the business you have undertaken, I shall endeavor to be particular & circumstantial.

1st. The care of negroes is the first thing to be recommended that you give me timely notice of their wants that they may be provided with all Necessarys: The Breeding wenches more particularly you must Instruct the Overseers to be Kind and Indulgent to, and not force them when with Child upon any service or hardship that will be injurious to them & that they have every necessary when in that condition that is needful for them, and the children to be well looked after and to give them every Spring & Fall the Jerusalem Oak seed for a week together & that none of them suffer in time of sickness for want of proper care.

Observe a prudent and watchful conduct over the overseers that they attend their business with diligence, keep the negroes in good order, and enforce obedience by the example of their own industry, which is a more effectual method in every respect of succeeding and making good crops than Hurry & Severity; The ways of industry are constant and regular, not to be in a hurry at one time and do nothing at another, but to be always usefully and steadily employed. A man who carries on business in this manner will be prepared for every incident that happens. He will see what work may be proper at the distance of some time and be gradually & leisurely providing for it, by this foresight he will never be in confusion himself and his business instead of a labor will be a pleasure to him.

2nd. Next to the care of negroes is the care of stock & supposing the necessary care taken, I shall only here mention the use to be made of them for the improvement of the Tobacco Grounds, Let them be constantly and regularly penned. Let the size of the Pens be 1000 Tobacco Hills for 100 Cattle, and so in proportion for a Greater or less Quantity, and the Pens moved once a week. By this practise steadily pursued a convenient quantity of land may be provided at Moss's neck without clearing, and as I intend this seat of land to be a settlement for one of my sons, I would be very sparing of the woods, and that piece of woods that lies on the left hand of the Ferry Road must not be cut down on any account. A proper use of the cattle will answer every purpose of making Tobacco without the disturbance too commonly made of the Timber land & as you will see this Estate once a Fortnight, you may easily discover if they have been neglectful of Pening the Cattle and moving the Cowpens.

Take an exact account of all the Negroes & Stocks at each Plantation and send to me; & Tho once a year may be sufficient to take this account yet it will be advisable to see them once a month at least; as such an Inspection will fix more closely the overseers' attentions to these points. As complaints have been made by the negroes in respect to their provision of Corn, I must desire you to put that matter under such a Regulation as your own Prudence will dictate to you; The allowance to be Sure is Plentiful and they ought to have their Belly full but care must be taken with this Plenty that no waste is Committed; You must let Hampton know that the care of the Negroes' corn, sending it to mill, always to be provided with meal that every one may have enough & that regularly and at stated times, this is a duty as much incumbent upon him as any other. As the corn at Moss's neck is always ready money it will not be advisable to be at much Expense in raising Hogs: the shattered corn will probably be enough for this purpose. When I receive your account of the spare corn At Moss's Neck and Richland which I hope will be from King and Queen Court, I shall give orders to Col. Tucker to send for it.

Let me be acquainted with every incident that happens & Let me have timely notice of everything that is wanted, that it may be provided. To employ the Fall & Winter well is the foundation of a successful Crop in the Summer: You will therefore Animate the overseers to great diligence that their work may be in proper forwardness and not have that to do in the Spring that ought to be done in the Winter: there is Business sufficient for every Season of the year and to prevent the work of one Season from interfering with the work of Another depends upon the care of the overseer.

The time of sowing Tobacco seed, the order the Plant Patch ought to be in, & the use of the Wheat Straw I have not touched upon, it being too obvious to be overlooked.

Supposing the Corn new laid & the Tobacco ripe for Housing: To cut the Corn Tops and gather the blades in proper time is included under the care of Cattle, their Preservation in the Winter depending upon Good Fodder. I shall therefore confine myself to Tobacco. Tobacco hogsheads should always be provided the 1st week in September; every morning of the month is fit for striking & stripping; every morning therefore of this month they should strike as much

Tobacco as they can strip whilst the Dew is upon the Ground, and what they strip in the morning must be stemmed in the Evening: this method Constantly practised, the Tobacco will be all prised before Christmas, weigh well, and at least one hogshead in Ten gained by finishing the Tobacco thus early. You shall never want either for my advice or assistance. These Instructions will hold good for Poplar Neck & Portobacco & perhaps Spotsylvania too.

I now send my two Carpenters Mack & Abram to Mosses Neck to build a good barn, mend up the Quarters & get as many staves and heading as will be sufficient for next years Tobacco hogshead. I expect they will compleat the whole that is necessary upon that Estate by the last of March. . . .

Even the hardest working people relax sometimes. The southern colonists chose a variety of ways, as Dr. John Brickell noted in The Natural History of North Carolina *(Dublin, 1737), pp. 37-42.*

The chiefest diversions here are fishing, fowling; and hunting wild beasts, such as deer, bears, racoons, hares, wild turkies, with several other sorts, needless to treat of here, 'till we come to describe each particular specie.

Horse-racing they are fond of, for which they have race-paths, near each town, and in many parts of the country. Those paths, seldom exceed a quarter of a mile in length, and only two horses start at a time, each horse has his peculiar path, which if he quits, and runs into the other, looses the race. This is agreed on to avoid jockying. These courses being so very short, they use no manner of art, but push on with all the speed imaginable; many of these horses are very fleet.

It is common for people to come and go from this province to Virginia, to these publick diversions.

They are much addicted to gaming, especially at cards and dice, hazard and all-fours, being the common games they use; at which they play very high, nay to such a pitch, that I have seen several hundred pounds won and lost in a short time.

Cock-fighting they greatly admire, which birds they endeavor to procure from England and Ireland, and to that intent, employ masters of ships, and other trading persons to supply them.

Wrestling, leaping, and such activities are much used by them; yet

I never observed any foot races. Dancing they are all fond of, especially when they can get a fiddle, or bagpipe; at this they will continue hours together, may, so attach'd are they to this darling amusement, that if they can't procure musick, they will sing for themselves. Musick, and musical instruments being very scarce in Carolina.

These are the most material observations I have made in respect of their usual diversions.

But they have a particular season, which is only at their wheat-harvest, not to be omitted; this they celebrate with great solemnity, it is the beginning of June—which time the planters notify to each other, that they design to reap the aforesaid grain, on a certain day, some send their Negroes to assist, others only go to partake of the great feasts, etc. Some will frequently come twenty, nay thirty miles on this occasion, the entertainments are great, and the whole scene pleasant and diverting; but if they can get musick to indulge this mirth, it greatly adds to the pleasure of the feast. It must be confest, that this annual revelling is very expensive to the planters, but as its customary, few omit it, nor have they ever those publick diversions at the reaping of any other grain but the European wheat.

III. LOVE AND MARRIAGE

Love knows no borders. Why did John Rolfe want to marry Pocahontas? What qualms did he have? Judging from his intentions, what qualms might she have had? What role did the Virginia gentry play in the marriages and married lives of their children? What did a southern man look for in a wife? Were southerners prudish in their behavior or conversation? What might explain this? How was sexual infertility regarded by the working classes?

The first and perhaps the greatest American love affair was that of John Rolfe, the young Virginia planter, and Pocahontas, the daughter of the powerful chieftain Powhatan. Rolfe's letter of 1614 to the deputy-governor of Virginia explaining his feelings is reprinted in Narratives of Early Virginia, 1606-1625, *edited by Lyon Gardiner Tyler (New York, 1907), pp. 239-244.*

The coppie of the Gentle-mans letters to Sir Thomas Dale, that after maried Powhatans daughter, containing the reasons moving him thereunto.

Honourable Sir, and most worthy Governor:
When your leasure shall best serve you to peruse these lines, I trust in God, the beginning will not strike you into a greater admiration, then the end will give you good content. It is a matter of no small moment, concerning my own particular, which here I impart unto you, and which toucheth mee so neerely, as the tendernesse of my salvation. Howbeit I freely subject my selfe to your grave and mature judgement, deliberation, approbation and determination; assuring my selfe of your zealous admonitions, and godly comforts, either

perswading me to desist, or incouraging me to persist therin, with a religious feare and godly care, for which (from the very instant, that this began to roote it selfe within the secret bosome of my brest) my daily and earnest praiers have bin, still are, and ever shall be produced forth with as sincere a godly zeale as I possibly may to be directed, aided and governed in all my thoughts, words and deedes, to the glory of God, and for my eternal consolation. To persevere wherein I never had more neede, nor (till now) could ever imagine to have bin moved with the like occasion.

But (my case standing as it doth) what better worldly refuge can I here seeke, then [than] to shelter my selfe under the safety of your favourable protection? And did not my ease proceede from an unspotted conscience, I should not dare to offer to your view and approved judgement, these passions of my troubled soule, so full of feare and trembling is hypocrisie and dissimulation. But knowing my owne innocency and godly fervor, in the whole prosecution hereof, I doubt not of your benigne acceptance, and clement construction. As for malicious depravers, and turbulent spirits, to whom nothing is tastful, but what pleaseth their unsavory pallat, I passe not for them being well assured in my perswasion (by the often triall and proving of my selfe, in my holiest meditations and praiers) that I am called hereunto by the spirit of God; and it shall be sufficient for me to be protected by your selfe in all vertuous and pious indevours. And for my more happie proceeding herein, my daily oblations shall ever be addressed to bring to passe so good effects, that your selfe, and all the world may truely say: This is the worke of God, and it is marvelous in our eies.

But to avoid tedious preambles, and to come neerer the matter: first suffer me with your patence, to sweepe and make cleane the way wherein I walke, from all suspicions and doubts, which may be covered therein, and faithfully to reveale unto you, what should move me hereunto.

Let therefore this my well advised protestation, which here I make betweene God and my own conscience, be a sufficient witnesse, at the dreadfull day of judgement (when the secret of all mens harts shall be opened) to condemne me herein, if my chiefest intent and purpose be not, to strive with all my power of body and minde, in the undertaking of so mightie a matter, no way led (so farre forth as mans weakenesse may permit) with the unbridled desire of carnall affection: but for the good of this plantation, for the honour of our countrie, for the glory of God, for my owne salvation, and for the converting to the true knowledge of God and Jesus Christ, an unbeleeving creature, namely Pokahuntas. To whom my hartie and best thoughts are, and have a long time bin so intangled, and inthralled in so intricate a laborinth, that I was even awearied to unwinde my selfe thereout. But almighty God, who never faileth his, that truely invocate his holy name hath opened the gate, and led me by the hand that I might plainely see and discerne the safe paths wherein to treade.

To you therefore (most noble Sir) the patron and Father of us in this countrey doe I utter the effects of this my setled and long continued affection (which hath made a mightie warre in my meditations) and here I doe truely relate, to what issue this dangerous combate is come unto, wherein I have not onely examined, but throughly tried and pared my thoughts even to the quicke, before I could finde any fit wholesome and apt applications to cure so daungerous an ulcer. I never failed to offer my daily and faithfull praiers to God, for his sacred and holy assistance. I forgot not to set before mine eies the frailty of mankinde, his prones[s] to evill, his indulgencie of wicked thoughts, with many other imperfections wherein man is daily insnared, and oftentimes overthrowne, and them compared to my present estate. Nor was I ignorant of the heavie displeasure which almightie God conceived against the sonnes of Levie and Israel for marrying strange wives, nor of the inconveniences which may thereby arise, with other the like good motions which made me looke about warily and with good circumspection, into the grounds and principall agitations, which thus should provoke me to be in love with one whose education hath bin rude, her manners barbarous, her generation accursed, and so discrepant in all nurtriture from my selfe, that oftentimes with feare and trembling, I have ended my private controversie with this: surely these are wicked instigations, hatched by him who seeketh and delighteth in mans destruction; and so with fervent praiers to be ever preserved from such diabolical assaults (as I tooke those to be) I have taken some rest.

Thus when I had thought I had obtained my peace and quietnesse, beholde another, but more gracious tentation hath made breaches into my holiest and strongest meditations; with which I have bin put to a new triall, in a straighter manner then the former: for besides the many passions and sufferings which I have daily, hourely, yea and in my sleepe indured, even awaking mee to astonishment, taxing mee with remisnesse, and carelesnesse, refusing and neglecting to performe the duetie of a good Christian, pulling me by the eare, and crying: why dost not thou indevour to make her a Christian? And these have happened to my greater wonder, even when she hath bin furthest seperated from me, which in common reason (were it not an undoubted worke of God) might breede forgetfulnesse of a farre more worthie creature. Besides, I say the holy spirit of God hath often demaunded of me, why I was created? If not for transitory pleasures and worldly vanities, but to labour in the Lords vineyard, there to sow and plant, to nourish and increase the fruites thereof, daily adding with the good husband in the Gospell, somewhat to the tallent, that in the end the fruites may be reaped, to the comfort of the laborer in this life, and his salvation in the world to come? And if this be, as undoubtedly this is, the service Jesus Christ requireth of his best servant: wo unto him that hath these instruments of pietie put into his hands, and wilfully despiseth to worke with them. Likewise, adding hereunto her great apparance of love to me, her desire to be taught and instructed in the knowledge of God, her capablenesse of understanding, her aptnesse and willingnesse to receive anie good impression, and also the spirituall, besides her owne incitements stirring me up hereunto.

What should I doe? shall I be of so untoward a disposition, as to refuse to leade the blind into the right way? Shall I be so unnaturall, as not to give bread to the hungrie? or uncharitable, as not to cover the naked? Shall I despise to actuate these pious dueties of a Christian? Shall the base feare of displeasing the world, overpower and with holde mee from revealing unto man these spirituall workes of the Lord, which in my meditations and praiers, I have daily made knowne unto him? God forbid. I assuredly trust hee hath thus delt with me for my eternall felicitie, and for his glorie: and I hope so to be guided by his heavenly graice, that in the end by my faithfull paines, and christianlike labour, I shall attaine to that blessed promise, Pronounced by that holy Prophet Daniell unto the righteous that bring many unto the knowledge of God. Namely, that they shall shine like the starres forever and ever. A sweeter comfort cannot be to a true Christian, nor a greater incouragement for him to labour all the daies of his life, in the performance thereof, nor a greater gaine of consolation, to be desired at the hower of death, and in the day of judgement.

Againe by my reading, and conference with honest and religious persons, have I received no small encouragement, besides *serena mea conscientia*, the cleerenesse of my conscience, clean from the filth of impurity, *quoe est instar muri ahenei*, which is unto me, as a brasen wall. If I should set down at large, the perturbations and godly motions, which have striven within mee, I should but make a tedious and unnecessary volume. But I doubt not these shall be sufficient both to certifie you of my tru intents, in discharging of my dutie to God, and to your selfe, to whose gracious providence I humbly submit my selfe, for his glory, your honour, our Countreys good, the benefit of this Plantation, and for the converting of one unregenerate, to regeneration; which I beseech God to graunt, for his deere Sonne Christ Jesus his sake.

Now if the vulgar sort, who square all mens actions by the base rule of their own filthinesse, shall taxe or taunt me in this my godly labour: let them know, it is not any hungry appetite, to gorge my selfe with incontinency; sure (if I would, and were so sensually inclined) I might satisfie such desire, though not without a seared conscience, yet with Christians more pleasing to the eie, and lesse fearefull in the offence unlawfully committed. Nor am I in so desperate an estate, that I regard not what becommeth of mee; nor am I out of hope but one day to see my Country, nor so void of friends, nor mean in birth, but there to obtain a mach to my great content: nor have I ignorantly passed over my hopes there, or regardlesly seek to loose the love of my friends, by taking this course: I know them all, and have not rashly overslipped any.

But shal it please God thus to dispose of me (which I earnestly desire to fulfill my ends before sette down) I will heartely accept of it as a godly taxe appointed me, and I will never cease, (God assisting me) untill I have accomplished, and brought to perfection so holy a worke, in which I will daily pray God to blesse me, to mine, and her eternall happines. And thus desiring no longer to live, to enjoy the blessings of God, then [than] this my resolution doth tend to such godly ends, as are by me before declared: not doubting of your favourable acceptance, I take my leave, beseeching Almighty God to raine downe upon you, such plenitude of his heavenly graces, as your heart can wish and desire, and so I rest,

At your commaund most willing
to be disposed off
JOHN ROLFE.

Among the many things that Landon Carter commented upon in his diary were the affairs of the heart of the Virginia gentry. The following excerpts come from his Diary, *edited by Jack P. Greene (Charlottesville, 1965).*

1770: 25 May. I went this day to Captain Beale's who gave his Son Thomas a public dinner upon the bringing home of his late married wife Miss [illegible Ball]. It is no business of mine but for a Lady so much talked of and for whom so many young fellows has pretended to run mad I think there is as little to be seen as ever I saw in any one. There is a silence but not graced with quite so much good humour as to bespeak the wisdom of it. One thing struck me. This Gentleman by his first wife had a couple of pretty Children neatly dressed playing about who seemed as if they wanted to be fondled by their new Mama but indeed She did not seem to take the least notice of them. Which to me would argue a want of prudence had she really a proper affection for certainly no woman willing to oblige her husband would according to the tenor of the Scripture have missed so fine an opportunity as the taking notice of one of these little ones must have been to engage her husband['s] affections. He passes for a phylosopher but I believe he is only happy in wanting the power of judging with propriety of such things for he seemed as if unobserving of this behaviour though it was really so contrary to natural prudence and conjugal love. There was a large Company there and I met the famous Hudson Muse going there of whom I took no notice always bearing in mind his opening and exposing private letters that did not in the least affect him.

1774: 25 May. Yesterday my Poor offending Child Judy came for the 1st time since she was deluded away to be unhappily married against her duty, my will, and against her Solemn Promise. And this too to a man unsound by birth as he descended from a man long before bedrid for months before his birth, which bad Stamen has once made its Appearance in a most corrupted case, only releived by an alarming fit of the Piles which for a while has checked Consumptive tendency; but such a Stamen seems only to be for a while contended against by the Youthfulness of his solids, which must give way Perhaps sooner than he thinks of; and how is such a creature to maintain a woman who has always lived well and delicately, with only a poor Pittance of an estate, a bit of land, and about 6 slaves? Indeed this fine girl has made a hard bed, such has been her deception. I will contrive that she shall not want for Personal necessaries, But I will give nothing, that either he or his inheritors can claim. I well remember the Case of his Namesake; the old Fox got all he had, whilst his widow got nothing and Paid his debts to boot.

Though I resolved not to let nature discover its weakness on seeing her; I was only happy in that I could burst into tears; a poor miserable girl, I could not speak to her for some time.

15 June. My daughter Judith went home to meet her husband, and as she came in by herself to my chamber when I was alone to take leave of me I told her that for very Prudent reasons perhaps too tender to tell her I had determined that whatever assistance she had from me everything should only be lent to her, to be returned to my Call, order, or appointment, how and when I should chuse, and this from under her husband's hands obligatory on him, heirs or assigns. That I did not chuse to do it for her life because that would constitute A Property in her husband during that time, and might be removed for debt or otherwise. That I knew the family she married into and that I was sure everything from thence would be convertable if any accident of death should happen and that she might be made a beggar by whom she least expected; for I now certainly knew by whom she had been deceived.

I then asked her if she was not breeding, she answered she was sure to the Contrary. I told her that without any desire to affect her or estrange the man she had Chosen for her companion; that she might be glad of that Circumstance; for as to his Stamen I was certain a person descended from so goutified a stock must be very bad and she would now find herself annoyed all the days of her and his life; and a child by such a man must be only a constant additional Concern. But of this she could only have been advised by her father who through the hypocrisy of her Aunt was never permitted to be heard by her. To this, she made no reply but kissed me and took leave of me.

1775: 10 September. On thursday last Mr. W[illiam] C[olston] came here and Communicated his intention of waiting on my daughter Lucy. I told him I had long entertained such a Suspicion and really with Pleasure for his Virtue and unexceptionable behaviour had long attached my good wishes to him. But as a Parent I never took any Liberty with a child but to dissuade where I thought I had reason so to do; but in no instance Whatever to Persuade. Therefore her approbation must Proceed from his own conduct and her good liking. I should give her £800 Sterling as soon as the times would admit of it.

1776: 9 January. When Mr. Colston had discovered how my daughter Lucy's affections lay, he ventured to speak to me, telling me he should have done it sooner, but he was doubtful as to the provisions in his entailed estates. I answered him I had only £800 sterling to give her as a portion (and would make a settlement upon her if Mr. Colston's entailed estate was restricted by the donor). Certainly, then, these must be deemed the terms of my consenting to the match. Accordingly, the wedding takes effect, and as soon as I saw Mr. Colston was desirous of carrying his wife home, I told him as I understood he wanted a few slaves to stock his plantation better, I intended the crop after this to give him 6 slaves which should be valued and their value to be received as a part of the £800 sterling. This he expressed a seeming desire should be done. Accordingly, I offered my wench Frankey, who used to wait on my daughter, to be taken as one. Lucy said there did not seem to be any occasion; the wench was a fine work woman and would be wanted to work for me as her mother was now in a measure past it. Therefore, she only desired Frankey for a few days till she could instruct Mr. Colston's girl intended for the house. This was, accordingly done and after 7 or 8 days the wench returned. At this visit my daughter told me she must take her word back again, and desired she might have Frankey on the terms I at first offered her. I agreed to this, as I found all parties willing; then I asked my daughter if she knew how Mr. Hornsby had given the house and land. She answered that Mr. Colston's widow, in case of such an accident, was somehow provided for, but could not tell how. Yesterday I communicated this conversation to Colston, adding that I wanted to be satisfied how by Mr. Hornsby's gift of the house, etc., his widow, possibly without children, was to be provided for; and he answered, she was only to be maintained out of that estate during her life. I then replyed that the negroes, at least, I should let him have as a part of her fortune ought to be settled upon his wife; and he then actually told me, to be sure it was most reasonable they should be so done, and begged that I would get such an instrument. I told him any lawyer could easily draw such an one and repeated to him the Purport of it. Our conversation ended with seeming satisfaction. But in the evening I discovered a dulness in him, and only asked if he was unwell, and was answered: No, he was very well. I said no more, believing his dulness was an effect of something natural in him. But this morning, when alone, he told me he was a little too hasty yesterday in consenting to the negroes being settled on his wife; for in such a case he said he should have no power over them to part with them as he might think proper; and his whole fortune might as well have been settled upon her, which he could not have done if I had at first demanded it; because he was in debt for a tract of adjoyning land which he had bought. I became serious, and spoke to this effect: Sir, I have treated you rather more like a gentleman than you at first did me, for you did not speak to me before you had engaged my daughter's affections, but, imputing this to love and bashfulness, I thought nothing about it, but did not my conversation about her fortune before marriage tend to know whether the donor of your estate had not restrained the law as to a widow's dower out of entailed lands; and did not that imply a settlement on my child, if you had told me then it did? How then, now you do tell me it does, can you wish I had demanded this settlement at first, because you would not have agreed to it? Was there an equal or a greater temptation to a parent in such a match in your estate, than there was in other Gentlemen's fortunes who have married my daughters? The gift to you, only saying your widow shall be maintained out of the estate given away to another, if you die without heirs must either leave my children in the power of others or of the law, and what would this differ from a Parent throwing his child into a river that some kind hand might save her from drowning? He then told me that his wife thought that there would be no manner of occasion for such a settlement. I answered she seemed to reason as he did on the present moment in the full shine of a honeymoon, but things of this sort should extend and could be only meant after his death, when, perhaps the moons of others might never shine on his widow. However, said I, don't disturb yourself. Your wife out of weakness might, seeing your uneasiness, tell you so; but no Prudent parent ought not to do so. But if you want to be at liberty to leave her a beggar, should you choose it, for God's sake do it. He offered then to leave the fortune in my hands. I replied no, Sir, no one shall ever have an opportunity of declaring anything with a face so interested as that must appear. I will let you have the 6 negroes the next crop, as I promised, and Frankey shall go now agreeable to your desire. He then asked me at what value? I began then to see, and replied, to be sure a very healthy wench and a fine workwoman must be of much more value than an outworker. And so our conversation ended.

It may be something, at this time, a little inconsiderate in this Gentleman, but I cannot help crowding myself into some doubts only to be trusted to myself, but I will be honest, and Prudent to boot. I can't but still condemn Lucy's too easy confidence in others; at the same time she seems to suspect her father, but before the God whom I now write, I mean nothing but a real Parental care; and may he so direct me and others. They went home this day. I think I every day see stronger reasons for my great caution in this world.

Tutor John Harrower at Belvidera, the estate of Colonel William Daingerfield, was also privy to match-making among the gentry. His acquaintance with Lucy Gaines, the young housekeeper of the estate, provided him with the following entries in his Journal, *edited by Edward Miles Riley (Williamsburg, 1963), pp. 118, 138-139.*

SUNDAY 24TH. [September 1775]

This day after dinner Miss Lucy put into my hands for my perusal a love letter she recd. while she was up the Country from a young man worth an Estate of £400. She hade not seen or heard from him for three Years befor. She says she does & always did hate him. As it is a curiosity I shall here insert it Verbatum and Just as it is adressed & spelled.

my deear love and the delite of my life very well remembur the great sattisfaction we have had in Each others Company but now is grone Stranger to Each other I understand you are a going to be marrid and I wish you a good husband with all my hart if you are ingaigd and if not I shuld think my self happy in making you mistress of my hart and of Evrething Els as I am worth if you culd have as much good will for me as I have for you we might live I belive very happy you may depend on my Cincerety If you think fit to Except of my offer I will make you my lawfull wife as sone as posoble if not I hope no harme don tho I can nevor forgit your preshus lips as I have Cist so offten and am very desiours to make them my one my Cind love and best respct to you my dove; this from your poor but faithfull lover till death PS pray let me no by the barer wheathar it is worth my while to put mysilf to the truble to com & see you or not

Aadressed To Mrs. Lewse Gains

Sunday 25th. [February 1776]

At Mr. Beck's with Miss Lucy. In the evening Mr. Frazer returned from his Mothers & made me a present of a new Cotton Handkierchiff worth 2/ of his Mother's spinning & weaving & hemed for me by his sister.

After we went to Bed I tuched upon his marriage with Miss Lucy. He asked me if [I] thought it wou'd be a match, I told him I did; And asked him if he did not think so himself. He answered me that he had a great many thoughts, That he was young & cou'd hardly maintain himself, That it was a Daingerous situation & ought to be well considered off, That he hade a fickle Master to do with & was uncertain of his time here, That at any rate he was determined not to stay above another year here, if he staid that. I told him that one in his Bussiness cou'd afford to live better married, than a man in any Other Bussiness whatever, & that if he was married a great many articles might be made in his house at a verry small expence which run away with a deale of money from him when he went to the store. That every one who seed her (if they did her Justice) must allow her to be a genteel, cliver, weel looked girle & of a good temper, and that I wou'd be greatly decieved in her if she did not make an extream good wife. He allowed her to be a verry good Girle, But added that while he was single, if he was affronted he cou'd move at pleasure, which was not so easy done when married, for that after marriage soon came somethin else (meaning Childreen) which was not so easily removed, when perhaps one did not know where to go too when out of Bussiness, I told him as to that he cou'd never be at a loss haveing a good place of his own to go to when he pleased, upon which he dropped the subject. Upon the whole, I find he either does not chuse to own to me, that he designs to marrie her, or is as yet unsettled upon it if he will have her for his wife or not: And as matters seems to stand fair betwixt them at present I do not think it prudent to aquant Miss Lucy with this conversation at least for some time; As I wou'd willingly avoide every word that might give offence upon either side as I sinceerly think them well deserving of each other.

Freiday 1st. March. [1776]

Miss Lucy in School all last night, which fretted Mrs. Daingerfield this day, because she was Obliged to sleep in the Nursery with Johnnie. At noon I hade a conversation with Lucy, When she told me she had a mind never to come more nigh the School. I told her she ought not to breack off coming all at once, But to confine herself to the houre of 10 or 11 at farthest, And if he insisted on her staying longer to desire him to Marrie at once, & then they cou'd be at their full freedom. Same time I told her not to build too strongly on him as the time proposed to finish the Bargain was far distant and he seemingly determined not to shorten it; Some time ago she asked him what answer he wou'd give me if I jested him on it. He answered, That he was courting Lucy & wou'd have her if he cou'd get her. Compare this with my conversation with Him 25th. Ulto.

When love descends to earth it sometimes winds up in the courts, as the County Court Records of Accomack-Northampton, Virginia, 1632-1640, *ed. Susie M. Ames (Washington, 1954), testify.*

1634: 8 September. [Present] mr. Obedyence Robins commander, mr. John How, mr. william Stonne, mr. william Burdett, mr. william Andrewes.

In the first place upon the complaynt of Phillip Taylor against John Little for abusinge his house in going to bed to the mayd of the syd Taylors, and the next day the syd Littell being at worke in the ground with a Company of men boasted that the Cooke [cock] was up, and the steale downe and reddy to give fyre, but as the syd Littell confesseth he was disturbed It is therefor ordered that the syd John Littell shall for the syd offence lay neck and Hyels close for 3 howres And for as much as the syd Littell confesseth himself to be drunk at that tyme, It is therefor ordered that for the syd offence he shall pay 5s according to a statute, unto Walter Scott provost marshall.

It is ordered that Ellen Muce for accusinge of John Littell to have to doe with her in the act of fornication and not approveinge the same, that she shalbe whipped.

At this Cort Edward Drew preferred a petition against Joane Butler for caling of his wife common Carted hoare and upon dew examination, and the deposition of John Holloway and William Baseley who affermeth the same on oath to be true that the syd Joane Butler used those words.

Upon dew examination it is thought fit by this board that the syd Joane Butler shall be drawen over the kings Creeke at the starne of a boate or Canew from on [one] Cowpen to the other, ore else the next saboth day in the tyme of devyne servis betwixt the first and second lesson present her selfe befor the minister and say after him as followeth. I Joane Butler doe acknowledge to have called Marie Drew hoare and thereby I confesse I have done her manefest wronge, wherfor I desire befor this congregation, that ye syd Marie Drew will forgive me, and alsoe that this congregation, will joyne, and praye with me, that God may forgive me.

Upon the petition of Thomas Butler against Marie the [wife of Edward] Drew for reportinge the syd Thomas to have to doe with Bridgett the wife of mr. John Wilkins in the act of adultery for which purpose Joane Muns Aged 30 yeares or ther abouts sworne and examined sayeth that Joane the wife of Thomas Butler told her goinge downe to the old Plantation togeather, that her husbound shewed her wher he layed the Head and heeles of Bridgett Wilkins, and that the syd Bridgett would have given him as much Cloth as would make him a shert, and this is all that this deponant can say.

15 September. Upon the petition of Thomas Butler against marie Drew for Calinge of his wife carted hoare, and that she saw the syd Thomas Butlers wife carted in England. It is therefor ordered upon the deposition of tow witnesses by this board that the syd Marie Drew shall aske the syd Thomas Butlers wife forgiveness in the Church on the next saboth day, presenting her selfe befor the minister betwext the first and second lesson and say after him as followeth I Mary Drewe doe acknowledge to have called Joane Butler carted hoare, and therby I confess I have done her manifest wrong, wherfor I desire befor this congregation that the syd Joane Butler will forgive me and alsoe that this congregation will joyne and

pray with me that God may forgive me, or else suffer the like punishment as the syd Joane Butler hath done.

3 November. Lewes Whyt oth [   ]

That while Edward Drew was at the Duck [   ] william Payne layd with his wife and had the [   ] six or seventh tymes all most every night that winter she told him. Alsoe she told him she was with Chyld by him and they knew not what to doe but Edward Drew coming [   ] knocked it in the head, Lewes askinge him how he came acquainted with her he answered, that drinking on[e] night with her layed his hand one her belly and told her he could make it as flatt as a pancake, the next morning he came ther, and she told him he was a man of words and not of deeds. Alsoe he sayd he would not have had any thing to doe with her, but he saw young Powell use ther and to put out him he thought to make use of her himselfe, then he came a little whyle after and would have layen with her, and she denied him he asked her the reason. She sayd noe body should lay with her he asked if he was not as well as young Powell she sayd noe, he was a younge man [and if] her husband should chance not to come home or dye then he was able to make her amends this is all that Lewes Whyt [can say].

1637: 25 September. The deposition of Elizabeth Neale the wife of Mr. John Neale

This deponent sayth that she taxeing Francis Millicent with cer[tain] opprobrious speeches he shold use against Mary Jolly, he answered that if she were not with child she was lately with child, and more she saith not.

The deposition of Henry Walker

This deponent saith that Francis Millicent told him that John Foster was in bed with Mary Jolly and that Elyas Hartrey and his wife wold say soe much as he the said Francis had told him, and that the said Elyas wife shold say to her husband, that if these things be suffered people will report that our house is a Bawdy house. And this is all he can say.

The deposition of Elyas Hartrey and Jane his wife

These deponents say that they neither knowe nor ever sawe any dishonesty by Mary Jolly.

Whereas it is made to appeare to this Courte by the depositions of severall partyes that Francis Millicent hath unjustly and wrongfully scandelized and defamed Mary Jolly servant to Mr. John Neale. It is therefore thought Fitt and soe ordered by this Courte that the said Francis Millicent shall be whipt and have thirty lashes and to aske the said Mary Jolly forgivenes publiquely in the Congregation the first Sabbath that she is able to come to Church and the said Millicent to pay the charges of the suite.

The deposition of Anne Wilkins the wife of John Wilkins

This deponent saith that Anne Williamson the wife of Roger Williamson and Anne Stephens the wife of Christopher Stephens came to the Cowe Pen and there did in a jeering manner abuse Grace Waltham saying that John Waltham husband of the said Grace hade his Mounthly Courses as Women have, and that the said Anne Stephens shold say that John Waltham was not able to gett a child. And further she saith not. Anne Stephens the wife of William Stephens, *idem*.

Upon the Complaynt of John Waltham against Anne Williamson the wife of Roger Williamson and Anne Stephens the wife of Christopher Stephens for abusing him the said John Waltham and his wife by most vyle and scandalous speeches.

It is therefore thought fitt and soe ordered by this Courte that the said Anne Williamson and Anne Stephens shalbe duckt, and shall aske the said John Waltham and his wife forgivenes in the publique Congregation.

The English—north or south, native or colonial—were fond of contracts. They drew them up as readily for God and marriage as they did for government and market. The following marriage contract is taken from the Archives of Maryland, *ed. J. Hall Pleasants (Baltimore, 1940), vol. 57, pp. 468-469.*

Articles of agreement, made and agreed upon between William Berry of the one part and Margaret Preston, both of Patuxent River in the County of Calvert, of the other part, witnesseth that the abovesaid Margaret Preston and William Berry have fully and perfectly concluded and agreed, that the said Margaret doth reserve for her own proper use and behoof, before she doth engage herself in marriage to the said William Berry, the value of one hundred pounds sterling, to be at her the said Margaret's own disposal, in such goods as shall be hereafter mentioned: viz.

Plate, to the value and worth of forty pounds sterling.

The little Negro girl called Sarah, born in Richard Preston's house, valued to ten pounds sterling. If the said girl should die, the said William Berry [agreed] to make the same good to the said Margaret by another Negro or the value.

A good mare to ride on, value seven pounds sterling.

A chamber or room to be well furnished with bedding and furniture, with other household stuff to the value of forty-three pounds sterling.

And for a further testimony that the abovementioned articles are fully and perfectly concluded and agreed upon by the parties aforesaid, the said William Berry both binds himself, his heirs, executors, and administrators to the true performance of all and every [one] of the abovementioned articles, to the full value as is aforementioned, whensoever the said Margaret Preston shall make demand of the same for her own proper use. But if it shall be so ordered after the aforementioned William Berry and Margaret Preston be married that the said William shall die first, that then the abovesaid goods (or the value) do remain firm to and for the said Margaret's own proper use, as she shall think fit to bestow, over and above her proportion of the estate which by the said William Berry shall be left her. For the true performance of this agreement the abovesaid William Berry hath hereunto set his hand and seal this ninth day of the tenth month, called December, in the year one thousand, six hundred, sixty, and nine.

William Berry (sealed)

Signed and Sealed
in presence of
  George Deulins
  Wm. Jones

Recorded at the instance and request of the abovenamed William Berry, January the 8th, 1669.

Marriage was not always a simple matter of economics and love in the colonial South. Having the ceremony performed was often a difficult task for many couples in the backcountry. Charles Woodmason, an itinerant Anglican preacher in the Carolinas, penned the "Remonstrance presented to the Common's House of Assembly of

South Carolina, by the Upper Inhabitants of the said Province Nov. 1767" which became the backbone of the Regulator Movement for political and social equality with the eastern shore towns. The following excerpt is taken from the remonstrance printed in The Carolina Backcountry on the Eve of Revolution: The Journal and Other Writings of Charles Woodmason, Anglican Itinerant, *ed. Richard J. Hooker (Chapel Hill, 1953), pp. 224-226.*

And no *Marriage Licence* can be obtain'd but in *Charlestown*—And there ev'ry Person must repair to get Married, that would marry judicially and according to Law—for We have not Churches wherein to publish Banns, or Ministers to Marry Persons, Wherefrom, the Generality marry each other, which causes the vilest Abominations, and that Whoredom and Adultery overspreads our Land. Thus We live and have liv'd for Years past as if without God in the World, destitute of the Means of Knowledge, without *Law* or *Gospel, Esteem*, or Credit. For, We know not even the Laws of this Country We inhabit for where are they to be found, but in the Secretarys Office in Charlestown? The Printing a Code of the Laws, hath been long petitioned for, often recommended by the *Crown*, and delineated in the *presentments of Grand Juries*, as a Matter long wanting, and of the utmost Consequence: But like all other their Presentments, it lyes *totally unregarded*.

Of what Service have been—Of what Use are the Parish Churches of *Prince George, Prince Frederic* and *St. Mark*, to the Inhabitants of Williamsburgh Great and Little Pedee, Lynchs Creek, Waccamaw, the Congarees, Waxaws, Waterees, Saludy, Long Canes, Ninety Six, or Broad River! Places and Settlements containing Fifty thousand Souls? These Fabrics were plac'd where they are, to serve some Local Occasion, or particular Persons or Purposes; But are not (at least at present) of the least Benefit to the Back Country: What Church can We repair too for Divine Service, nearer than *Dorchester* or *Charlestown?* Several Parishes being now destitute of Ministers, and no effectual Plan settled for their being properly supplied.

It is notorious, That thro' the Want of Churches and Ministers, New Sects have arisen, now greatly prevail, especially those call'd *New Lights*. Prophaneness and Infidelity abound—Ignorance, Vice, and Idleness prevail—And to the Great Indifference shewn by all Ranks to promote the Interests of Religion and Vertue, it is in Great Measure owing that such few Checks have been given to the *Villains* and *Outlaws*, who have devour'd Us. For, the Common People hardly know the first Principles of Religion: And so corrupt are their Morals, that a Reformation of Manners among them *in our Time* is more to be wish'd for than expected.

Thro' want of Churches and Ministers, many Persons go into the *North* Province, there to be Married, by Magistrates; Which hath encouraged many of our Magistrates (so venal are they) for to take on them also to solemnize Marriages—And this, without any previous Publication of Banns or any Sett Form, but each after his own Fancy, which occasions much Confusion, as they ask no Questions, but couple Persons of all Ages, and ev'ry Complexion, to the Ruin, and Grief of many families. Their Example have been followed by the Low Lay Teachers of ev'ry petty Sect, and also copied by *Itinerant* and Stragling Preachers of various Denominations, who traverse the Back Country, (sent this Way from *Pennsylvania* and *New England*, to poison the Minds of the People)—From these irregular Practices, the sacred Bond of Marriage is so greatly slighted, as to be productive of many Great and innumerable Evils. For many loose Wretches are fond of such Marriages; On Supposition, that they are only Tempor[ar]y, or *Durante Placito*; Dissoluble, whenever their Interests or Passions incite them to Separate. Thus they live *Ad Libitum*; quitting each other at Pleasure, Inter-Marrying Year after Year with others; Changing from Hand to Hand as they remove from Place to Place, and swapping away their Wives and Children, as they would Horses or Cattle. Great Scandal arises herefrom to the Back Country, and Loss to the Community: For the Issue of such are too often expos'd deserted, and disown'd: Beggars are hereby multiplied—Concubinage establish'd (as it were) *by Law;* The most sacred Obligations are hereby trampled on, and Bastardy, Adultery, and other heinous Vices become so common, so openly practic'd and avow'd as to lose the Stigma annex'd to their Commission: These are some of the Main Roots from whence the reigning Gangs of Horse Theives have sprung up from.

IV. RIGHT AND WRONG

Every society reflects itself in its laws. What do the laws and court cases of the South reveal about the lives and living conditions of the colonists? about their Indian neighbors? What was the procedure of law from indictment to judgement in the courts? Ideally, was the law executed without regard to person? In actuality, was the administration of justice unequal? Why? Was the South "puritanical"? in what ways? Why?

The first laws governing Virginia were made by the military leaders of the Virginia Company, but in 1619 the government of the colony was transferred to a General Assembly resident in Jamestown. There the governor, Sir George Yeardley, six councillors, and twenty burgesses—two from each of the ten settlements—met to pass the first body of laws by a legislative assembly on the American continent. The result of their work is printed in Narratives of Early Virginia 1606-1625, *ed. Lyon Gardiner Tyler (New York, 1907), pp. 262-274.*

Here begin the lawes drawen out of the Instructions given by his Maties Counsell of Virginia in England to my lo: la warre, Captain Argall and Sir George Yeardley, knight.

By this present General Assembly be it enacted that no injury or oppression be wrought by the English against the Indians whereby the present peace might be disturbed and antient quarrels might be revived. And farther be it ordained that the Chicohomini are not to be excepted out of this lawe; untill either that suche order come out of Englande or that they doe provoke us by some newe injury.

Against Idlenes, Gaming, drunkenes and excesse in apparell the Assembly hath enacted as followeth:

First, in detestation of Idlenes be it enacted, that if any man be founde to live as Idler or renagate, though a freedman, it shalbe lawful for that Incorporation or Plantation to which he belongeth to appoint him a Mr [Master] to serve for wages, till he shewe apparant signes of amendment.

Against gaming at dice and Cardes be it ordained by this present assembly that the winner or winners shall lose all his or their winninges and both winners and loosers shall forfaite ten shillings a man, one ten shillings whereof to go to the discoverer, and the rest to charitable and pious uses in the Incorporation where the faulte is comitted.

Against drunkenness be it also decreed that if any private person be found culpable thereof, for the first time he is to be reprooved privately by the Minister, the second time publiquely, the thirde time to lye in boltes 12 howers in the house of the Provost Marshall and to paye his fee, and if he still continue in that vice, to undergo suche severe punishment as the Governor and Counsell of Estate shall thinke fitt to be inflicted on him. But if any officer offende in this crime, the first time he shall receive reprooff from the Governour, the second time he shall openly be reprooved in the churche by the minister, and the third time he shall first be comitted and then degraded. Provided it be understood that the Governor hath alwayes power to restore him when he shall in his discretion thinke fitte.

Against excesse in apparell that every man be cessed in the churche for all publique contributions, if he be unmarried according to his owne apparell, if he be married, according to his owne and his wives, or either of their apparell.

As touching the instruction of drawing some of the better disposed of the Indians to converse with our people and to live and labour amongst them, the Assembly who knowe well their dispositions thinke it fitte to enjoin, least to counsell those of the Colony, neither utterly to reject them nor yet to drawe them to come in. But in case they will of themselves come voluntarily to places well peopled, there to doe service in killing of Deere, fishing, beatting of Corne and other workes, that then five or six may be admitted into every such place, and no more, and that with the consente of the Governour. Provided that good guarde in the night be kept upon them for generally (though some amongst many may proove good) they are a most trecherous people and quickly gone when they have done a villany. And it were fitt a house were builte for them to lodge in aparte by themselves, and lone inhabitants by no meanes to entertain them.

Be it enacted by this present assembly that for laying a surer foundation of the conversion of the Indians to Christian Religion, eache towne, citty, Borrough, and particular plantation do obtaine unto themselves by just means a certinc number of the natives' children to be educated by them in true religion and civile course of life—of which children the most towardly boyes in witt and graces of nature to be brought up by them in the first elements of litterature, so to be fitted for the Colledge intended for them that from thence they may be sente to that worke of conversion.

As touching the busines of planting corne this present Assembly doth ordain that yeare by yeare all and every householder and householders have in store for every servant he or they shall keep, and also for his or their owne persons, whether they have any Servants or no, one spare barrell of corne, to be delivered out yearly, either upon sale or exchange as need shall require. For the neglecte of which duty he shalbe subjecte to the censure of the Governor and Counsell of Estate. Provided always that the first yeare of every newe man this lawe shall not be of force.

About the plantation of Mulbery trees, be it enacted that every man as he is seatted upon his division, doe for seven yeares together, every yeare plante and maintaine in growte six Mulberry trees at the least, and as many more as he shall think conveniente and as his vurtue and Industry shall move him to plante, and that all suche persons as shall neglecte the yearly planting and maintaining of that small proportion shalbe subjecte to the censure of the Governour and the Counsell of Estate.

Be it farther enacted as concerning Silke-flaxe, that those men that are upon their division or setled habitation doe this next yeare plante and dresse 100 plantes, which being founde a comodity, may farther be increased. And whosoever do faill in the performance of this shalbe subject to the punishment of the Governour and Counsell of Estate.

For hempe also both English and Indian and for English flax and Anniseeds, we do require and enjoine all householders of this Colony that have any of those seeds to make tryal thereof the nexte season.

Moreover be it enacted by this present Assembly, that every

householder doe yearly plante and maintaine ten vines untill they have attained to the art and experience of dressing a Vineyard either by their owne industry or by the Instruction of some Vigneron. And that upon what penalty soever the Governor and Counsell of Estate shall thinke fitt to impose upon the neglecters of this acte.

Be it also enacted that all necessary tradesmen, or so many as need shall require, suche as are come over since the departure of Sir Thomas Dale, or that shall hereafter come, shall worke at their trades for any other man, each one being payde according to the quality of his trade and worke, to be estimated, if he shall not be contented, by the Governor and officers of the place where he worketh.

Be it further ordained by this General Assembly, and we doe by these presents enacte, that all contractes made in England between the owners of the lande and their Tenants and Servantes which they shall sende hither, may be caused to be duely performed, and that the offenders be punished as the Governour and Counsell of Estate shall thinke just and convenient.

Be it established also by this present Assembly that no crafty or advantagious means be suffered to be put in practise for the inticing awaye the Tenants or Servants of any particular plantation from the place where they are seatted. And that it shalbe the duty of the Governor and Counsell of Estate most severely to punish both the seducers and the seduced, and to returne these latter into their former places.

Be it further enacted that the orders for the Magazin [storehouse] lately made be exactly kepte, and that the Magazin be preserved from wrong and sinister practises, and that according to the orders of courte in Englande all Tobacco and sasafras be brought by the Planters to the Cape marchant till suche time as all the goods nowe or heretofore sent for the Magazin be taken off their hands at the prices agreed on. That by this meanes the same going for Englande with one hande the price thereof may be uphelde the better. And to that ende that all the whole Colony may take notice of the last order of Courte made in Englande and all those whom it concerneth may knowe howe to observe it, we holde it fitt to publishe it here for a lawe among the rest of our lawes. The which order is as followeth:

Upon the 26 of October, 1618, it was ordered that the Magazin should continue during the terme formerly prefixed and that certaine abuses now complained of should be reformed and that for preventing of all Impositions save the allowance of 25 in the hundred proffitt, the Governor shall have an invoice as well as the Cape Marchant, that if any abuse in the sale of the goods be offered, wee upon Intelligence and due examination thereof, shall see it correctede. And for incouragement of particular hundreds, as Smythe's hundred, Martin's hundred, Lawnes' hundred, and the like, it is agreed that what comodoties are reaped upon anie of these General [several] Colonies, it shalbe lawfull for them to returne the same to their owne adventurers. Provided that the same comodity be of their owne growing, without trading with any other, in one entyre lumpe and not dispersed and that at the determination of the jointe stocke, the goods then remaining in the Magazin shalbe bought by the said particular Colonies before any other goods which shall be sente by private men. And it was moreover ordered that if the lady la warre, the Lady Dale, Captain Bargrave and the rest, would unite themselves into a settled Colony they might be capable of the same priviledges that are graunted to any of the foresaid hundreds. Hitherto the order.

All the general Assembly by voices concluded not only the acceptance and observation of this order, but of the Instruction also to Sir George Yeardley next preceding the same. Provided first, that the Cape Marchant do accepte of the Tobacco of all and everie the Planters here in Virginia, either for Goods or upon billes of Exchange at three shillings the pounde the beste, and 18d the second sorte. Provided also that the billes be only payde in Englande. Provided, in the third place, that if any other besides the Magazin have at any time any necessary comodity which the Magazine dothe wante, it shall and may be lawfull for any of the Colony to buye the said necessary comodity of the said party, but upon the termes of the Magazin viz: allowing no more gaine then 25 in the hundred, and that with the leave of the Governour. Provided lastly, that it may be lawfull for the Governor to give leave to any Mariner, or any other person that shall have any suche necessary comodity wanting to the Magazin to carrie home for Englande so muche Tobacco or other naturall comodities of the Country as his Customers shall pay him for the said necessary comodity or comodities. And to the ende we may not only persuade and incite men, but inforce them also thoroughly and loyally to aire their Tobacco before they bring it to the Magazine, be it enacted, and by these presents we doe enacte, that if upon the Judgement of fower sufficient men of any incorporation where the Magazine shall reside, (having first taken their oaths to give true sentence, twoe whereof to be chosen by the Cape Marchant and twoe by the Incorporation), any Tobacco whatsoever shall not proove vendible at the second price, that it shall there imediately be burnt before the owner's face. Hitherto suche lawes as were drawen out of the Instructions.

Tuesday, Aug. 3, 1619.

This morning a thirde sorte of lawes (suche as might proceed out of every man's private conceipt) were read and referred by halves to the same comitties which were from the beginning.

This done, Captaine William Powell presented to the Assembly a pettiton to have justice against a lewde and trecherous servante of his who by false accusation given up in writing to the Governor sought not only to gett him deposed from his government of James citty and utterly (according to the Proclamation) to be degraded from the place and title of a Captaine, but to take his life from him also. And so out of the said Petition sprang this order following:

Captaine William Powell presented a pettition to the generall Assembly against one Thomas Garnett, a servant of his, not onely for extreame neglect of his business to the great loss and prejudice of the said Captaine, and for openly and impudently abusing his house, in sight both of Master and Mistress, through wantonnes with a woman servant of theirs, a widdowe, but also for falsely accusing him to the Governor both of Drunkennes and Thefte, and besides for bringing all his fellow servants to testifie on his side, wherein they justly failed him. It was thought fitt by the general assembly (the Governour himself giving sentence), that he should stand fower dayes with his eares nayled to the Pillory, viz: Wednesday, Aug. 4th, and so likewise Thursday, fryday, and Satturday next following, and every of those dayes should be publiquely whipped. Now, as touching the neglecte of his worke, what satisfaction ought to be made to his Mr for that is referred to the Governour and Counsell of Estate.

The same morning the lawes abovewritten, drawen out of the instructions, were read, and one by one thoroughly examined, and then passed once again the general consente of the whole Assembly.

This afternoon the comitties brought in a reporte, what they had done as concerning the thirde sorte of lawes, the discussing whereof spente the residue of that daye. Excepte onely the consideration of a pettiton of Mr. John Rolfes againste Captaine John Martine for writing a letter to him wherein (as Mr. Rolfe alledgeth) he taxeth him both unseemly and amisse of certaine thinges wherein he was never faulty, and besides, casteth some aspersion upon the present government, which is the most temperate and juste that ever was in this country, too milde indeed, for many of this Colony, whom unwoonted liberty hath made insolente and not to know themselves. This Petition of Mr. Rolfes' was thought fitt to be referred to the Counsell of State.

Wednesday, Aug. 4th.

This daye (by reason of extream heat, both paste and likely to ensue and by that meanes of the alteration of the healthes of diverse of the general Assembly) the Governour, who himself also was not well, resolved should be the last of this first session; so in the morning the Speaker (as he was required by the Assembly) redd over all the lawes and orders that had formerly passed the house, to give the same yett one reviewe more, and to see whether there were any thing to be amended or that might be excepted againste. This being done, the third sorte of lawes which I am nowe coming to sett downe, were read over [and] thoroughly discussed, which, together with the former, did now passe the laste and finall consente of the General Assembly.

A thirde sorte of lawes, suche as may issue out of every man's private conceipte.

It shalbe free for every man to trade with the Indians, servants onely excepted, upon paine of whipping, unless the Mr. will redeeme it off with the payment of an Angell, one-fourth parte whereof to go to the Provost Marshall one forth parte to the discoverer, and the other moyty to the publique uses of the Incorporation.

That no man doe sell or give any of the greatter howes [hoes] to the Indians, or any English dog of quality, as a mastive, greyhound, bloodhounde, lande or water spaniel, or any other dog or bitche whatsoever, of the Englishe race, upon paine of forfaiting 5s sterling to the publique uses of the Incorporation where he dwelleth.

That no man do sell or give any Indians any piece shott or poulder, or any other armes, offensive or defensive upon paine of being held a Traytour to the Colony, and of being hanged as soon as the facte is proved, without all redemption.

That no man may go above twenty miles from his dwellingplace, nor upon any voiage whatsoever shalbe absent from thence for the space of seven dayes together without first having made the Governor or comaunder of the same place acquainted therwith, upon paine of paying twenty shillings to the publique uses of the same Incorporation where the party delinquent dwelleth.

That no man shall purposely goe to any Indian townes, habitations or places or resortes without leave from the Governor or comaunder of that place wher he liveth, upon paine of paying 40s to publique uses as aforesaid.

That no man living in this Colony, but shall between this and the first of January nexte ensueing come or sende to the Secretary of Estate to enter his own and all his servants' names, and for what terme or upon what conditions they are to serve, upon penalty of paying 40s to the said Secretary of Estate. Also, whatsoever Mrs or people doe come over to this plantation that within one month of their arrivall (notice being first given them of this very lawe) they shall likewise resorte to the Secretary of Estate and shall certifie him upon what termes or conditions they be come hither, to the ende that he may recorde their grauntes and comissions, and for how long time and upon what conditions their servants (in case they have any) are to serve them, and that upon paine of the penalty nexte above mentioned.

All Ministers in the Colony shall once a year, namely, in the moneth of Marche, bring to the Secretary of Estate a true account of all Christenings, burials and marriages, upon paine, if they faill, to be censured for their negligence by the Governor and Counsell of Estate; likewise, where there be no ministers, that the comanders of the place doe supply the same duty.

No man, without leave of the Governor, shall kill any Neatt cattle whatsoever, young or olde, especially kine, Heyfurs or cow-calves, and shalbe careful to perserve their steers and oxen, and to bring them to the plough and such profitable uses, and without having obtained leave as aforesaid, shall not kill them, upon penalty of forfaiting the value of the beast so killed.

Whosoever shall take any of his neighbors' boates, oares, or canoas without leave from the owner shalbe helde and esteemed as a felon and so proceeded againste; tho hee that shall take away by violence or stelth any canoas or other thinges from the Indians shall make valuable restitution to the said Indians, and shall forfaiet, if he be a freeholder, five pound; if a servant, 40s, or endure a whipping; and anything under the value of 13d shall be accounted Petty larcency.

All ministers shall duely read divine service, and exercise their ministerial function according to the Ecclesiastical lawes and orders of the churche of Englande, and every Sunday in the afternoon shall Catechize suche as are not yet ripe to come to the Com[munion]. And whosoever of them shalbe found negligent or faulty in this kinde shalbe subject to the censure of the Governor and Counsell of Estate.

The Ministers and Churchwardens shall seeke to presente all ungodly disorders, the comitters wherofe if, upon goode admontions and milde reprooff, they will not forbeare the said skandalous offenses, as suspicions of whordomes, dishonest company keeping with weomen and suche like, they are to be presented and punished accordingly.

If any person after two warnings, doe not amende his or her life in point of evident suspicion of Incontincy or of the comission of any other enormous sinnes, that then he or shee be presented by the Churchwardens and suspended for a time from the churche by the minister. In which Interim if the same person do not amende and humbly submit him or herself to the churche, he is then fully to be excomunicate and soon after a writt or warrant to be sent from the Governor for the apprehending of his person ande seizing on all his goods. Provided alwayes, that all the ministers doe meet once a quarter, namely, at the feast of St. Michael the Arkangell, of the nativity of our saviour, of the Annuntiation of the blessed Virgine, and about midsomer, at James citty or any other place where the Governor shall reside, to determine whom it is fitt to excomunicate, and that they first presente their opinion to the Governor ere they proceed to the acte of excomunication.

For the reformation of swearing, every freeman and Mr. of a family after thrise admontion shall give 5s or the value upon present demaunde, to the use of the church where he dwelleth; and every servant after the like admontion, excepte his Mr. discharge the fine, shalbe subject to whipping. Provided, that the payment of the fine notwithstanding, the said servant shall acknowledge his faulte publiquely in the Churche.

No man whatsoever, coming by water from above, as from Henrico, Charles citty, or any place from the westwarde of James citty, and being bound for Kiccowtan, or any other parte on this side, the same shall presume to pass by, either by day or by night, without touching firste here at James citty to knowe whether the Governor will comande him any service. And the like shall they performe that come from Kicawtan ward, or from any place between this and that, to go upwarde, upon paine of forfaiting ten pound sterling a time to the Governor. Provided, that if a servant having had instructions from his Master to observe this lawe, doe notwithstanding, transgresse the same, that then the said servant shalbe punished at the Governor's discretion; otherwise, that the master himselfe shall undergo the foresaid penalty.

No man shall trade into the baye, either in shallop, pinnace, or ship, without the Governor's license, and without putting in security that neither himself nor his Company shall force or wrong the Indians, upon paine that, doing otherwise, they shalbe censured at their returne by the Governor and Counsell of Estate.

All persons whatsoever upon the Sabaoth daye shall frequente divine service and sermons both forenoon and afternoon, and all suche as beare armes shall bring their pieces swordes, poulder and shotte. And every one that shall transgresse this lawe shall forfaicte three shillinges a time to the use of the churche, all lawful and necessary impediments excepted. But if a servant in this case shall wilfully neglecte his Mr's comande he shall suffer bodily punishmente.

No maide or woman servant, either now resident in the Colonie or hereafter to come, shall contract herselfe in marriage without either the consente of her parents, or of her Mr or Mris, or of the magistrate and minister of the place both together. And whatsoever minister shall marry or contracte any suche persons without some of the foresaid consentes shalbe subjecte to the severe censure of the Governor and Counsell of Estate.

Be it enacted by this present assembly that whatsoever servant hath heretofore or shall hereafter contracte himselfe in England, either by way of Indenture or otherwise, to serve any Master here in Virginia and shall afterward, against his said former contracte depart from his Mr without leave, or, being once imbarked shall abandon the ship he is appointed to come in, and so, being lefte behinde, shall putt himselfe into the service of any other man that will bring him hither, that then at the same servant's arrival here, he shall first serve out his time with that Mr that brought him hither and afterward also shall serve out his time with his former Mr according to his covenant.

Here ende the lawes.

Robert Beverley described the operation of the judicial system in his History and Present State of Virginia *(London, 1705), ed. David Freeman Hawke (Indianapolis, 1971), pp. 130-133.*

They have two sorts of courts that differ only in jurisdiction, namely, the general court and the county courts. I don't mention the court of admiralty, of which there is neither judge nor any salary appointed for him; and indeed upon these terms no man of any rank or abilities would care to undertake such a troublesome office. Neither is there the least occasion of any such charge, because their county courts sitting so frequently have hitherto supplied their place; and upon extraordinary occasion of dispatch in maritime affairs, the first justice in commission is authorized by law to call courts out of course to determine them.

The general court is a court held by the governor and Council who by custom are the judges of it in all civil disputes, but in all criminal cases they are made judges by the charter.

This court, as it did from the beginning so it does still, takes cognizance of all causes—criminal, penal, ecclesiastical, and civil. From this court there is no appeal except the thing in demand exceed the value of three hundred pounds sterling; in which case an appeal is allowed to the queen and Council in England and there determined by a committee of the Privy Council called the Lords of Appeals; the like custom being used for all the other plantations. In criminal cases I don't know that there's any appeal from the sentence of this court, but the governor is authorized to pardon persons found guilty of any crime whatsoever except of treason and willful murder, and even in those cases he may reprieve the criminal if the court represent him to be an object of mercy; which reprieve stands good and may be continued until her Majesty's pleasure be signified therein.

This court is held twice a year, beginning on the 15th of April and on the 15th of October. Each time it continues eighteen days, excluding Sundays, if the business hold them so long. And these are the only times of jail delivery.

The officers attending this court are the sheriff of the county wherein it sits and his under-officers. Their business is to call the litigants and the evidences into court and to impanel juries. But each sheriff in his respective county makes arrests and returns the writs to this court.

The way of impaneling juries to serve in this court is thus: The sheriff and his deputies every morning that the court sits goes about the town summoning the best of the gentlemen who resort thither from all parts of the country. The condition of this summons is that they attend the court that day to serve upon the jury (it not being known whether there will be occasion or no), and if any cause happen to require a jury they are then sworn to try the issue, otherwise they are in the evening, of course, dismissed from all further attendance, though they be not formally discharged by the court. By this means are procured the best juries this country can afford, for if they should be summoned by writ of venire from any particular county, that county cannot afford so many qualified persons as are here to be found because of the great resort of gentlemen from all parts of the colony to these courts as well to see fashions as to dispatch their particular business. Nor is visinage necessary there to distinguish the several customs of particular places, the whole country being as one neighborhood and having the same tenures of land, usages, and customs.

In criminal matters this method is a little altered, because a knowledge of the life and conversation of the party may give light to the jury in their verdict. For this reason a writ of venire issues in such cases to summon six of the nearest neighbors to the criminal, who must be of the same county wherein he lived; which writ is returned by the sheriff of the respective county to the secretary's office, and the names are taken from thence by the sheriff attending the general court and put in the front of the panel, which is filled up with the names of the other gentlemen summoned in the town to be of the petty jury for the trial of that criminal. If the prisoner have a mind to challenge the jurors, the same liberty is allowed him there as in England; and if the panel fall short by reason of such challenge, it must then be made up of the bystanders.

All actions are in that country brought to a determination the third court at farthest unless some special extraordinary reason be shown why the party can't make his defense so soon. The course is thus: Upon the defendant's nonappearance, order goes against the bail (for a *capias* is always their first process) on condition that unless the defendant appear and plead at the next court judgment shall then be awarded for the plaintiff. When the defendant comes to the next court he is held to plead, and if his plea be dilatory and overruled, he is held to plead over immediately. And if it can be the merits are tried that court, but the next it is ended without fail, except something happen to make it highly unreasonable. Thus a year and half ends a cause in the general court and three months in the county court. If anyone appeal from the judgment of the county court, the trial always comes on the succeeding general court, so that all business begun in the county court, tho' it runs to the utmost of the law (without some extraordinary event), is finished in nine months.

Everyone that pleases may plead his own cause or else his friends for him, there being no restraint in that case nor any licensed practitioners in the law. If anyone be dissatisfied with the judgment of the county court, let it be for any sum, little or great, he may have an appeal to the next general court, giving security to answer and abide the judgment of that court. But an action cannot originally be brought in the general court under the value of ten pounds sterling or of two thousand pounds of tobacco.

The county courts are constituted by commission from the governor with advice of Council. They consist of eight or more gentlemen of the county called justices of the peace, the sheriff being only a ministerial officer. This court is held monthly and has jurisdiction of all causes within the county not touching life or member, but in the case of hog stealing they may sentence the criminal to lose his ears, which is allowed by a particular act for that purpose. In all things they proceed in the same manner as the general court.

Besides this monthly court there is a day appointed to be kept annually by the justices of the said court for the care of all orphans and of their estates, and for the binding out and well ordering of such fatherless children who are either without any estate or have very little.

At these courts they inquire into the keeping and management of the orphan as to his sustenance and education. They examine into his estate and the securities thereof—if the sureties continue to be responsible, if his lands and plantations be kept improving and in repair, etc. If the poor orphan be bound an apprentice to any trade, then their business is to inquire how he is kept to his schooling and trade; and if the court find he is either misused or untaught they take him from that master and put him to another of the same trade or of any other trade which they judge best for the child.

Another charitable method in favor of the poor orphans there is this: That besides their trade and schooling the masters are generally obliged to give them at their freedom cattle, tools, or other things to the value of five, six, or ten pounds, according to the age of the child when bound, over and above the usual quantity of corn and clothes. The boys are bound till one and twenty years of age and the girls till eighteen. At which time they who have taken any care to improve themselves generally get well married and live in plenty, tho' they had not a farthing of paternal estate.

Though these courts be yearly appointed for that use, yet the justices do not fail every county court, as occasions happen, to do everything that can be for the benefit of orphans.

The colonial South was more English than "Southern," if by that is meant leisurely, rich, and indolent—the popular conception of the planter class of the antebellum South. And in the colonial period "English" meant hard-working, Protestant with a Calvanistic tinge, and future-oriented. Thus North Carolina's acts for the "Restraint of Vagrants" (1755). and for the "Better Observation and Keeping of the Lord's Day, Commonly Called Sunday; and for the More Effectual Suppression of Vice and Immorality" (1741). They are printed in the State Records of North Carolina, *vol. 23, pp. 173-175, 435-437.*

An Act for the Restraint of Vagrants

I. Whereas divers idle and disorderly persons, having no visible estates or employments, and who are able to work, frequently stroll from one county to another, neglecting to labor; and either failing altogether to list themselves as taxables, or by their idle and disorderly life, rendering themselves incapable of paying their levies, when listed: For remedy thereof,

II. Be it Enacted by the Governor, Council, and Assembly and by the authority of the same, that it shall not be lawful for any inhabitants of this government, to entertain, hire, or employ, in his or her house, above the space of forty eight hours, any such person or persons whatsoever, being taxable, and removing from the parish where he or she formerly resided, unless such person shall first produce a certificate, under the hand of the sherrif, or some magistrate of the county from whence he or she came, that such person paid levy there for the preceding year, or that he or she came into this government since, or was a servant at the time of taking the last list of taxables; and if any one shall entertain, hire, or employ, any such person or persons whatsoever, being taxable, not having such certificate as aforesaid, he or she so offending, shall forfeit and pay twenty shillings, proclamation money, for every such offence, to the informer; recoverable before any justice of the peace of the county where the offence shall be committed: and if any taxable person, not having such certificate, shall be liable to the like penalty of twenty shillings, proclamation money, to be recovered and applied as aforesaid.

III. And be it further enacted, by the authority aforesaid, that all able bodied persons, not having wherewithal to maintain themselves, who shall be found loitering and neglecting to labour for reasonable wages: all persons who run from their habitations, and have wives and children, without suitable means for their subsistence, whereby they are like to become burthensome to the parish wherein they inhabit; and all other idle, vagrant, or dissolute persons, wandering abroad, without betaking themselves to some lawful employments, or honest labour, or going about begging, shall be deemed rogues and vagabonds.

IV. And be it further enacted, by the authority aforesaid, that if any such vagabonds shall be found in any county or place, wandering, begging or misordering him or herself, it shall be lawful for any justice of the peace of that county, and he is hereby impowered and required, by warrant under his hand, to cause such vagabonds to be brought before him, and to examine and inform himself, as well by the oath and examination of the person apprehended, as of any other person or persons which oath or oaths the justice is hereby impowered to administer, and by any other ways or means he shall think proper, of the condition and circumstances of the person or persons so apprehended; and if it shall appear that he or she is under the description of vagabonds within this act, the said justice shall, by his warrant, order and direct him or her to be conveyed and whipt, in the same manner as runaways are, from constable to constable, to the county wherein his wife or children do inhabit, or where he or she did last reside (as the case may be) and there delivered to a justice of the peace, who is hereby required to cause every such vagabond to give sufficient security for his or her good behavior, and for betaking him or herself to some lawful calling, or honest labour; and if he or she fail so to do, then to commit him or her to the common goal of the county, there to remain until such security be given, or until the next court; which court is hereby impowered, if no security be then offered, to bind such vagabond to service, on wages for the term of one year; and such wages, after deducting the charges of the prosecution, and necessary cloathing, shall be applied towards supporting the family of such servant (if any) or otherwise paid to the person so bound after his or her time of service is expired, in full of all other recompence or reward: But if any such vagabond be of such evil repute, that no person will receive him or her into service, in such case the court shall order him or her to receive thirty nine lashes on his or her bare back, well laid on, at the public whipping post, and then to be discharged; and in both cases every such vagabond shall be guilty as aforesaid; and when any such vagabond shall be brought before a justice of the peace and it shall not appear to the said justice that he or she has acquired a legal settlement in any parish the said justice is hereby required to cause such vagabonds to give security for his or her good behavior, and for betaking him or herself to some honest calling or employment; and on failure thereof, shall commit him or her to the jail of the county, there to remain and be dealt with as is before herein directed.

An Act for the Better Observation and Keeping of the Lord's Day, Commonly Called Sunday; and for the More Effectual Suppression of Vice and Immorality

I. Whereas in well regulated governments, effectual care is always taken that the day set apart for publick worship, be observed and kept holy, and to suppress vice and immorality: Wherefore,

II. We pray that it may be enacted, and be it enacted, by his Excellency Gabriel Johnston, Esq., Governor, by and with the advice and consent of his Majesty's Council, and General Assembly of this province, and it is hereby enacted, by the Authority of the same, that all and every person and persons whatsoever shall, on the Lord's Day, commonly called Sunday, carefully apply themselves to the duties of religion and peity and that no tradesman, artificer, planter, labourer or other person whatsoever, shall, upon the Land or Water, do or exercise any labour, business or work, of their ordinary callings (works of necessity and charity only excepted), nor employ themselves either in hunting, fishing or fowling, or use any game, sport, or play on the Lord's Day aforesaid or any part thereof, upon pain that every person so offending, being of the age of fourteen years and upwards, shall forfeit and pay the sum of ten shillings, proclamation money.

III. And be it further enacted, by the authority aforesaid, that if any person or persons shall prophanely swear or curse, in the hearing of any justice of the peace, or shall be convicted of prophanely swearing and cursing, by the oath of one or more witness or witnesses, or confession of the party before any justice or justices of the peace, every such offender shall forfeit and pay the sum of the two shillings and six pence, of the like money, for every oath or curse. And if any person executing any public office, shall prophanely swear or curse, being first convicted, as aforesaid, such person shall forfeit and pay the sum of five shillings, of the like money, for each and every oath or curse.

IV. And be it further enacted, that if any person or persons shall prophanely swear or curse, in the presence of any court of record in this government, such offender or offenders shall immediately pay the sum of ten shillings, of the like money, for each and every oath or curse: to be deposited in the hands of the chairman of the said court and by him accounted for and paid, as hereinafter is directed: or to sit in the stocks, not exceeding three hours, by order of such court.

V. And be it further enacted, by the authority aforesaid, that every person convicted of drunkeness, by view of any justice of the peace, confession of the party, or oath of one or more witness or witnesses, such person so convicted shall, if such offence was committed on the Lord's Day, forfeit and pay the sum of five shillings of the like money; but if on any other day, the sum of two shillings and six pence, for each and every such offence.

IX. And be it further enacted, by the authority aforesaid, that if any persons commit fornication, upon due conviction, each of them shall forfeit and pay twenty five shillings proclamation money, for each and every such offence: to be recovered and applied to the same use as the other fines in this act.

X. And be it further enacted, that any two justices of the peace upon their own knowledge, or information made to them, that any single woman within this county is big with child, or delivered of a child or children, may cause such woman to be brought before them, and examine her, upon oath, concerning the father: and if she shall refuse to declare the father, she shall pay the fines in this act before mentioned, and give sufficient security to keep such child or children from being chargeable to the parish, or shall be committed to prison, until she shall declare the same, or pay the fine aforesaid, and give security as aforesaid. But in case such woman shall, upon oath, before the said justices, accuse any man of being the father of a bastard child or children, begotten of her body, such person so accused shall be adjudged the reputed father of such child or children, and stand charged with the maintenance of the same, as the county court shall order, and give security to the justices of the said court to perform the said order, and to indemnify the parish where such child or children shall be born, free from charges for his, or her, or their maintenance, and may be committed to prison until he find security for the same if such security is not by the woman before given.

XI. And be it further enacted, that the two said justices of the peace, at their discretion, may bind, to the next county court, him that is charged on oath, as aforesaid, to have begotten a bastard child, which shall not be then born, and the county court may continue such person upon security until the woman shall be delivered, that he may be forthcoming when the child is born.

XII. And be it further enacted, by the authority aforesaid, that this act shall be publicly read, two several times in the year, in all Parish churches and chappels, or for want of such, in the place where divine service is performed in every parish immediately after divine service; that is to say, on the first or second Sunday in April, and on the first or second Sunday in September, under the penalty of twenty shillings, proclamation money, for every such omission or neglect: to be levied by a warrant from a justice, and applied to the use of the parish where the offence shall be committed: and the church wardens of every parish are herby required to provide a copy of this act, at the charge of the parish.

The administration of justice in the South protected the small as well as the great. The following cases describe the accountability of masters to their servants and slaves; an equal number of cases, of course, could be produced to describe the wrong-doing of the other parties. The first case is the transcript of a trial that was transferred from a lower county court to the provincial court of Maryland. The defendant, Joseph Fincher, was eventually hanged for his crime. It is taken from the Archives of Maryland, *vol. 49, pp. 303-314. The second case also comes from the* Archives of Maryland, *vol. 41, pp. 190-191.*

*At a Provincial Court Held at St. Mary's
December 21, 1664*

Present: Charles Calvert, Esq., Governor
Philip Calvert, Esq., Chancellor
Mr. Baker Brooke

[The following is a transcript of Anne Arundel County Court Proceeding.]

Wee whose names are hereunder written being required to view the body of Jeffrey Hagman, servant to Joseph Fincher and to the best of our knowledge to returne our verdict how he came by his death, wee being sworne and having viewed the said Hagman's body doe finde no mortall wound about him that did occasion his death but doe unanimously concurr and judge the said Hagman being a diseased person died of the scurvey and an imposthume.

Witness our handes, August the 28th 1664

THOMAS BESSON, foreman	DENNIS N MACCONAH'S marke
ROBERT FRANCKLIN	WILLIAM W∃ GRAYE'S marke
JOHN GRAY	JOHN ∽ JONES' marke
ANDREW ROBERTS	JOHN KERSSEAKE
ROBERT LLOYDE	THOMAS TP PARSON'S marke
MAREN DUVALL	THEO. LEWYS

A true copy, witness myself, Theo. Lewys, Clerk of the Court, Anne Arundel

[*Writ*] *to Captain William Burges, Sheriff of Anne Arundel County*

Wee the commissioners Justices of the County of Anne Arundel doe hereby deliver unto you the body of Joseph Fincher who is suspected have murthered his servant Jeffrey Hagman, by the examination of severall witnesses.

These are therefore in the Lord Proprietor's name to will and require you to take him into Goale and there to keep him safe untill he be cleared by the law hereof. Fayle not as you will answer the contrary at your perill.

Given under our handes September 14th 1664

ROBERT BURLE	ROGER GROSE
THOMAS BESSON	RICHARD EWEN
RALPH WILLIAMS	JOHN NORWOOD

*At a Court Held for Anne Arundel County,
September 13, 1664*

Present Robert Burle	Capt. Thomas Besson	Commissioners
Roger Grose	Capt. John Norwood	[Justices]
Richard Ewen	Ralph Williams	

Edward Ladd aged 21 yeares or thereabouts sworne in court deposeth as followeth:

That he saw Joseph Fincher strike his servant but not in the tobacco house and those blowes that the said Fincher did at that time give his servant this deponent is sure could doe him no hurt, and further saith not.

EDWARD ◯ LADD his marke

Thomas Whyniard aged 21 yeares or thereabouts sworne in court deposeth as followeth:

That he saw Joseph Fincher strike his servant with a small sticke but not in the tobacco howse and further this deponent saith not.

THOMAS T WHYNIARD'S marke

Sussannah Leeth aged 20 yeares or thereabouts sworne in court deposeth as followeth:

This deponent going to worke saw Joseph Fincher pegging of plants and he called his man out worke, he not comming when he call'd him, he goes in and fetches him and loades him with a burden of plants. The man not able to beare them, the said Fincher followes him and flings him downe plants and all and beate him and kicked him and afterwards sent him into the howse. His wife turnes him back againe and sends him for a paile of water, she following him for another, and goeing to the spring the fellow not goeing soe fast as she would have him, she shuveth him along till he fell downe and afterwards she pull'd him up againe and gave him some blowes. Then coming from the springe the man fell downe with the paile in his hand, but this deponent knowes not whether there was any water in it or noe. She could not gett him up but calls to her husband. The man seeing his master comming getts up and goes toward the howse. His master followeth him and beateth him with a sticke. A while after wee came out againe to worke picking up plants wee heard a great noise in the tobacco howse whereof Joseph Fincher cryed; "gett up, gett up." A while after this deponent saw a little girle belonging to the howse rinning to the dwelling house and presently after Thomas Whyniard and fetch a bottle of dramms. My master seeing him runn calls to Lawrence Organ and goes to the tobacco house and further saith not.

Susanna Leeth

William Gunnell ages 22 yeares or thereabouts sworne in court deposeth as followeth:

That upon Fryday being the night before Joseph Fincher's man died this deponent saw the said Fincher loade his man with plants and loaded soe much on him that the said servant told his master he could not beare it, who said to his servant, "Sirrah doe or else I will beate you never was dogg soe beaten," who answered his master, "Master I cannot cary them allthough you knock me in the head," and the fellow staggering his master comming to him, kickt him and beate him with his fist saying, "Sirrah, Ille use thee never noe dogg was soe used. Ile either knocke thee in the head or starve thee rather than Ile lead this life with thee," and then Fincher called his servant to him againe and loaded him with some of the plants. The fellow carryed them as well as he could to the old howse. This was done on Fryday night before the fellow dyed. And the next morning this deponent being pegging of plants saw the said Fincher beate his servant againe with a sticke and likewise his fist and all soe kicked him and after this deponent went home and comming out againe from breakfast this deponent saw the said Fincher's wife and the fellow goeing to the spring. The fellow not goeing so fast as she would have him shuved him along and struck him with her hands and haul'd him & pull'd him and gott him up againe and comming from the springe the fellow fell downe againe and she call'd to her husband, and told him that she could not gett the fellow up. Her husband comming, the fellow rise and after he went up to the tobacco howse in the corne feilde and this deponent heard a greate noise and the fellow cryed out, "Lord, Master, if you beate me any more you will knock me in the head," and after this deponent saw a wench goeing downe to the dwelling howse. She not comming soe soon as they expected Thomas Whyniard runn after and brought up a bottle of dramms. Thomas Miles, this deponent's master seeing of him runn called to Lawrence Organ and told him that he thought in his heart the fellow was dead. And this deponent further saith that Joseph Fincher formerly reported he had beate his servant and brake 2 tobacco stickes about the sides of him and declared it to John Kickseeck, Lawrence Organ, and this deponent being in the feilde when the said Kickseeck spoke of it. This Joseph Fincher declared to the Dutchman and the Dutchman to us, and further saith not.

WILLIAM GUNNELL'S marke

Lawrence Organ aged 35 yeares or thereabouts sworne in court deposeth as followeth:

This deponent saw Joseph Fincher beate his servant with his hand and kickt him with his feete and likewise saw the said Fincher's servant's nostrills of his nose bloody in the house where he was dead and further saith not.

LAWRENCE LO ORGAN'S marke

Thomas Miles aged 45 yeares or thereabouts sworne in court deposeth as followeth:

This deponent being in the feilde saw Joseph Fincher loading of plants upon his man, he being not able to carry them, fell downe plants and all, and Joseph Fincher loaded his maid, soe when she was gone he ran to the fellow saying, "Can you neither carry plants nor walke," turn'd him home. His wife meeting of him turn'd him back againe till he came to the tobacco howse or thereabouts. There the fellow would goe noe further but fell downe. She called to her husband and told him the fellow would not walke. He, the said Fincher throwing downe the said plants that was in his armes and runn up to the tobacco howse and tooke up a stick and gave him foure or five blowes and kickt him and cufft him againe. Then about the 2nd or 3rd hour of the day this deponent being in the feilde with his people heard a greate noise in the tobacco howse like the clatterring of sticks and crying, "Gett up, gett up, why doe you not gett up," soe presently after this deponent saw the wench running home and after her Thomas Whyniard, seeing these thinges this deponent pondering in his minde what was the matter and it rise in his hart that the fellow was dead. Presently this deponent called Lawrence Organ and told him what he thought, who answered your deponent, "Come, let's goe and see," soe when we came to the tobacco howse dore wee saw the fellow upon the ground leaning against his master's knee, he being blooddy about the nose. This deponent askt Joseph Fincher how it came, who answered this deponent that he fell downe against the tobacco sticks and further this deponent saith not.

THOMAS MILES

A true copy, witness myself, Theo. Lewys, Clerk of the court, Anne Arundel county

Record of Trial in the Provincial Court

EXAMINATIONS TAKEN BEFORE THE
GOVERNOR AND COUNCIL

Joseph Fincher confess that Jeffrey Hagman dyed on the 27th day of August 1664.

Thomas Miles being further examined upon oath saith that when he came into the tobacco howse the said Jeffrey Hagman was dead and further saith he saw black spotts upon his body and hinder parts. Joseph Fincher was urgent with the said Myles to bury him before any body saw him and further saith that upon report he was beaten with 2 tobacco sticks by the said Joseph Fincher.

Lawrence Organ further saith that the very same day he dyed he saw the said Joseph Fincher beat the aforesaid Hagman.

Susanna Leeth further examined saith in the beginning of her deposition the words relates to the day that Jeffrey Hagman was slaine, and by these words he called his man Jeffrey Hagman was ment and by the words heard a greate noyse like the rattling of tobacco stickes.

William Gunnell further examined saith, being askt what Fincher's mans name was he saith Jeffrey, which said Jeffrey is since dead, Fincher and two freemen pegging of plants and saith he saw Thomas Whyniard come out of the howse and he goeing into the howse presently found the said Jeffrey dead.

Robert Loyde, surgeon, sworne saith being demanded if he viewed the body of the deceased person answered yes, and being demanded if he did see blew spots upon the forepart and hinder parts, answered, "yes, I saw two stroakes and a sore on his side that was formerly under my cure. . . . ."

Let it be inquired for the Right Honorable the Lord Proprietary whether Joseph Fincher in Rhode River in the county of Anne Arundel the 27th day of August in the yeare of our Lord God 1664 in the river and county aforesaid upon Jeffrey Hagman, servant to the said Joseph Fincher, by force and arms an assault did make and with certaine sticks of no vallue which he the said Joseph Fincher in his right hand then and there did hold, divers blowes on the body of the said Jeffrey Hagman did strike, soe that of the said blowes the said Jeffrey Hagman the day aforesaid did dye and soe if the said Joseph Fincher the said Jeffrey Hagman then and there feloniously and of malice forethought did kill and murder, contrary to the peace of his said Lordship his rule and dignity.

WILLIAM CALVERT

The witnesses names
  SUSANNA LEETH
  THOMAS MILES
  The mark of WILLIAM Z GUNNELL
  The mark of LAWRENCE LO ORGAN

The [grand] jurors having theire charge given departs the court by themselves to consider of the indictment with the evidences.

The jurors returnes into court answering all to theire names being demanded who should speake for them, answered the foreman, who delivers theire verdicts endorsed on the bills. . . .

On Joseph Fincher: A true bill. Uppon which the said prisoner was call'd to the barre and the presentment read to which the said Joseph Fincher pleads not guilty. Hee being demanded how he would be tryed, answered by God and his country.

The presentment as followeth:

The jury for the Right Honorable the Lord Proprietary doe present Joseph Fincher of Rhode River in the county of Anne Arundel, for that the said Joseph Fincher on the 27th day of August 1664 upon Jeffrey Hagman servant to the said Joseph Fincher in his right hand then and there did hold, divers blowes on the body of the said Jeffrey Hagman did strike soe that of the said blowes the said Jeffrey Hagman the day aforesaid dyd dye,

And soe the said Joseph Fincher the said Jeffrey Hagman then and there feloniously and of malice forethought did kill and murder contrary to the peace of his said Lordship his rule and dignity. . . .

Summons to sherriffe to impannell 12 good men and able for the petty jury. Sheriffe returns his writt and warrant:

Foreman Samuel Chew	John Watkins
Francis Holland	Philip Allumbey
Robert Peca	John Bayley
John Burrage	Robert Blinckhorne
Samuel Garland	Thomas Hopkins
John Ewen	William Evans

The indictment againe read, and the evidences called, examined, and sworne as before sett downe.

The jurors withdrew to consider of the said bille with the charge. They returne and being called answered every one to his name. The foreman delivers in theire verdict endorsed on the back side of the bill with this word (viz.) Guilty.

The prisoner call'd to the barre. Joseph Fincher hold up thy hand.

Are you agreed of your verdict? Answer: yes.

Who shall say for you? Answer: the foreman Mr. Samuell Chew.

Gentlemen of the jury, you say Joseph Fincher is guilty of the murder whereof hee stands indicted? Answered: yes.

You all say soe? Answer: Yes.

Joseph Fincher hold up thy hand. You doe remember upon your indictment you have been arraigned and have pleaded not guilty and for your tryall you have put your selfe upon God and country, which country hath found you guilty, for cann you now say for your selfe, why according to law you should not have judgment to suffer death? What saist thou, Joseph Fincher? Answered: that if he deserv'd it, he must dye. Being askt if there bee all he hath to say for himselfe, answered yes.

The judge gives sentence in these words following:

Joseph Fincher, you shall be carried to the place from whence you came, from thence to the place of execution, and there be hanged by the neck till you are dead. . . .

[To the High Sheriffe of the County of Anne Arundel]

These are in the name of the Right Honorable the Lord Proprietary of this province to will and require you to see the body of Joseph Fincher (who att our last court of session held at St. Mary's the 22nd of this instant December was arraigned and convicted of murder) carryed to the place of execution within three dayes after your receiving the said Fincher into your custody, and betwixt 8 and 9 of the clock in the morning there to hang by the neck till he be dead according to the judgment given on the day abovesaid, and for soe doeing this shall be your warrant.

Given under my hand this 27th day of December 1664

CHARLES CALVERT
[Governor]

[To the High Sheriffe of Anne Arundel County]

Whereas Thomas Whyniard and Edward Ladd late of your said county, planters, hath been arrested for suspition of felony by them as is said committed, wee will and command you therefore to receive into your custody the said Thomas Whyniard and Edward Ladd there to remaine untill by due course of law they shall be delivered.

Witness our deare brother Philip Calvert, Esq., Chancellor of our province of Maryland.

Given att St. Mary's this 23d day of December 1664.

PHILIP CALVERT

*Att a Provincial Court Held att St. Clement's Manor,
December 2, 1658*

Present: Josias Fendall, Esq., Governor
Philip Calvert, Esq., Secretary
Thomas Gerard
Col. John Price
Thomas Cornwalleys, Esq.

ATTORNEY GENERAL V. OVERZEE

Mr. William Barton informes the court against Mr. Symon Overzee, for that the said Overzee correcting his negro servant the said negro dyed under his said correction.

The examination of Hannah Littleworth aged 27 yeares or thereabouts taken the 27th of November 1658, before Philip Calvert, Esq.

This Examinant sayth that sometime (as shee conveives) in September was two yeares, Mr. Overzee commanded a negro (commonly called Tony) formerly chayned up for some misdemeanors by the command of Mr. Overzee (Mr. Overzee being then abroad) to be lett loose, and ordered him to goe to worke, but instead of goeing to worke the said negro layd himselfe downe and would not stirre. Whereupon Mr. Overzee beate him with some peare tree wands or twiggs to the bigness of a man's finger att the biggest end, which hee held in his hand, and uppon the stubbernes of the negro caused his dublett to be taken of, and whip'd him uppon his bare back, and the negro still remayned in his stubbernes, and feyned himselfe in fitts, as hee used att former times to doe. Whereuppon Mr. Overzee commanded this examinant to heate a fyre shovel, and to bring him some lard, which shee did, and sayth that the said fyre shovel was hott enough to melt the lard, but no soe hot as to blister anyone, and that it did not blister the negro, on whom Mr. Overzee powr'd it. Immediately thereuppon the negro rose up, and Mr. Overzee commanded him to be tyed to a Ladder standing on the foreside of the dwelling howse, which was accordingly done by an Indian slave, who tyed him by the wrist, with a piece of a dryed hide, and (as shee remembers but cannot justly say) that hee did stand uppong the grownd. And still the negro remayned mute or stubborne, and made noe signes of conforming himselfe to his masters will or command. And about a quarter of an howre after, or less, Mr. Overzee and Mrs. Overzee went from home, and [she] doth not know of any order Mr. Overzee gave concerning the said negro. And that while Mr. Overzee beate the negro and powred the lard on him, there was nobody by, save only Mr. Mathew Stone, and Mrs. Overzee now deceased. And that from the time of Mr. Overzee and his wife going from home, till the negro was dead, there was nobody about the howse but only the said Mr. Mathew Stone, William Hewes, and this examinant, and a negro woman in the quartering house, who never stir'd out. And that ofter Mr. Overzee was gone, uppon the relation of Mr. Mathew Stone, in the presence of William Hewes that the negro was dying, this examinant desyred Mr. Mathew Stone to cutt the negro downe, and hee refused to doe it, William Hewes allso bidding him let him alone and within lesse than halfe a howre after the negro dyed, the wind comming up att northwest soone after hee was soe tyed, and hee was tyed up betweene three and fowre o'clock in the afternoone, and dyed about six or seaven, and was kept till next morning before he was buried.

Uppon the reading this examination (Hannah Littleworth being present in court) when shee came to that particular concerning the tying of the negro up by the wrists (viz) Whither hee stood uppon the grownd Yea or Noe? Shee declareth that now shee very well remembers that hee stood uppon the grownd.

William Hewes sworne in upon court sayth that hee was present, att the time when Mr. Overzee beate the negro, and saw him allso powre lard uppon him, and that as hee conceaves and remembers, he saw noe blood drawne of the negro, and this deponent being willing to help the negro from the grownd, Mr. Overzee haveing his knife in his hand, cutting the twigs, threatened him to runne his knife in him (or words to that effect) if he molested him, and that the negro (as he thinks, but cannot justly say) stood uppon the grownd, and sayth further that the negro did commonly use to runne away, and absent himselfe from his Mr. Overzees service.

The governor requests the councell, then present, to declare their opinions, whither it was in the power of the court to judge this business now, Yea or noe? Mr. Overzee humbly requesting the court to end it, and that he may be acquitted, and uppon consideration that Mr. Mathew Stone was allsoe present as is declared whose examination is not yett taken, may evidence some things materiall in the business, it is agread by the board, and ordered that Mr. Overzee putt in bond of one hundred pownds of tobacco, to the Lord Proprietary for his appearance att the next Provinciall Court, and there to attend the finall determination of the same.

Although the great and the small were equal before the law, the law was not always equally distant from those who needed it. Charles Woodmason's letter to John Rutledge of South Carolina in defense of the demands of the backcountry Regulators underlines some of the inequalities. It is taken from The Carolina Backcountry on the Eve of the Revolution, *ed. Richard J. Hooker (Chapel Hill, 1953), pp. 272-278.*

This Copy of a letter sent to J. R. Esq. by the Regulators.

Sir

You say, that it is very Impertinent and Invidious for the Back Inhabitants to call themselves *Slaves*, When no People on Earth are in so great a State of freedom—and that they turn their Liberty into Licentiousness—And You ask with what Consistency or Propriety they presume to use the Word Slavery, in the Advertisement posted up at the Exchange.

You also say That our Legislature and Executive Powers have done for us all Services which we merit, or require, even beyond our deserts—and shewn us ev'ry possible Mark of Kindness and Goodness—but that we take too much upon us.

Whatever You in Town may fix as the Criterion of Things We, who *Know* and *Feel* where the Shoe pinches, can best determine. We think our Selves in a State of Servitude and those who are so, what other can they be denominated than Slaves?

You say, that a *Great deal* hath been *done* for us, and much more than We *Merit*—If so, then much remains *undone* (as I shall note presently) to bring us on the same Level (which You want not) the same foot with Your Selves . . .

But We will put our Selves Sir into Your Hands; and as Your Genius and Capacity is allow'd to be as Great as your avarice Be pleas'd (for once without a Fee) to consider the following Queries—and then say, if the Term *Slavery*, be unapplicable to us.

(1) Is it not *Slavery*, for to travel 2, or 300 Miles, to sue for a Debt

of 21 Pounds (3 £ Sterling), and for to spend, six, nay ten Times that Sum, Law Charges, in Recovery of it? Exclusive of Time, Labour, Application, and Travelling Expences?

(2) Is [it] not *Slavery*, for an Officer to come with a Writ (like a Letter de Cachet) and force us *in a Moment*, from our Dwelling—Not give us a Minute to settle our Affairs, send for our friends—Compound the Debt, or look about us, but must be hurried in an instant 200 Miles down to C.T. there thrown into a stinking Goal, and lye many Months—While at same time, we know not the Party who arrests us—Or never had any Accounts or dealings with him—Or heard of Him—Or if any Connexions, possibly he may be ours, not we his Debtor—And all this we must suffer except we can raise Bail for 10 days—Then that Bail must surrender us in Town—where we must instantly go to Goal, if we cannot raise Special Bail—Which not one in an hundred can do in Town, where they are unknown And possibly not one in an hundred in the Country will be accepted should they ride 200 Miles down to Town with us—To Goal we must Go—And possibly after all this, the Party may discontinue—Never try the Cause—while we lye rotting in a filthy Dungeon—And after all this Suffering, and being put to vast Expence, We can have no Reparation—No Redress for such Usuage—The greatest Stranger in the Country who never saw us, may treat any one in this Manner; In England there is 24 Hours granted to the Party before he can be moved to Prison—but here, not a Minute? In [Is] nothis [not this] as great Slavery as if we liv'd in France?

2]Is it not Slavery, that when a Writ goes against me, I should oft times not know ought of the Matter—and Execution be awarded—That my Lands shall be seized and sold in C. T. unknown to me—and for Nothing—tho' of great Value—That my Slaves shall be taken and carried down there, and sold for not one tenth of their Value; Ev'rything I have took Possession off by the Provost Marshall And thus for satisfying a Debt of 100 £ —I shall have Effects sold worth 1—2—Pounds: Many Instances of which can be given.

(3) Is it not Slavery to be supenead to Court as a Witness, and travel 2 or 300 Miles—stay for days together in C. T. at great Expence—and never call'd on? The like when summon'd as a Juror—and in many other Instances!

(4) Is it not Slavery for to be imprison'd fetter'd arraign'd, put on Trail [*sic*] on Allegation or Information of some Villain, or by

Malice of some Mean Justice of Peace—and no Prosecutor appear against me—No Prosecutor too be found to sue for false imprisonment or to get any Redress for Loss of Liberty Credit Fame and Fortune? Yet this often happens to many.

(5) Is it not Slavery to travel 2 or 300 Miles to procure a Licence to be married or have Banns publish'd, or my Child Christen'd or to hear a Sermon, or receive the Holy Communion—? And as for Churching of Women—Visiting the Sick, Burial of the Dead, and other Spiritual Offices we are entirely destitute, there being neither Church or Minister among us.

(6) Is it not Slavery to travel 50, or 60 Miles to find a Magistrate, for to make a single Affadavit, or sue for a small Debt Or for to be sued before Magistrates, who never saw, or know any thing of the Provincial, or Common Laws?

7)—Is it not Slavery to ride such Lengths to appear as Evidence in some trifling nonsensical Suit, between two fools, about Matters not worth six pence While it shall cost me Ten Pounds Expence beside Loss of Time?

8) Is it not Slavery to ride 200 Miles to give my Vote for Election of Vestry Men—Church Wardens—Members of Assembly &c or to get any Parochial Business transacted?

9)—Is it not Slavery to be burthen'd with Vagrants—Poor Travellers Sick—Infirm—Aged Diseased, Lame Persons, Orphans and others who by Choice or Accident push or force themselves on me and whom it is impossible to remove without breach of the Laws of Charity, Humanity, and Christianity—There being no Workhouse—Hospital, Bridewell, or provision made, or the least Relief establish'd in these Parts for Objects of Charity, Paupers, Orphans &c.

10) Is it not Slavery to leave my Estate and Children behind me in hands of Executors and Trustees, who shall spend my Estate during the Minority of my Children—give them no Education—and when of Age, perhaps bring them in Debt? for Want of an Orphan Law?

11) Is it not Slavery for to be at the Time and Cost of 2 or 300 Miles to assist the Civil Officer, in conveying of Criminals to Goal?
And for poor People, who quitted their Native Land where they lived Easily and decently, for to come here to be Beggars—to be employ'd in cutting down the Woods and clearing Lands to raise Crops—and afterwards for to be obliged to cut Roads, to carry their Produce to

Market—If any Peasants in Russia, Poland or Germany are in a worse State of Servitude than this, then Sir we will join You in that pious Wish You made in the House That the Back Country was at Bottom of the Sea.

V. HEAVEN AND EARTH

The church is earthly as well as heavenly. What were the chief problems of the Virginia clergy? How do they compare with those of the ministers in Carolina? How did each react to their situation? What does belief in witchcraft reveal about a society? Are they at peace with themselves socially or spiritually? How could a witch be recognized? What does an outbreak of evangelism reveal about a society? What were the consequences of New Light evangelism in Carolina? Was there a profound change in people's lives?

Virginia adhered to the Church of England, establishing one island of religious stability in the southern sea of denominational evangelism. Robert Beverley described the temporal arrangements of the church in The History and Present State of Virginia *(London, 1705), ed. David Freeman Hawke (Indianapolis, 1971), pp. 134-136, while Andrew Burnaby, a visiting Anglican minister, analyzed one of its chief problems in his* Travels through the Middle Settlements in North-America in the Years 1759 and 1760 *(2nd ed. London, 1775; reprinted Ithaca, 1960), pp. 17-21.*

Their parishes are accounted large or small in proportion to the number of tithables contained in them and not according to the extent of land. They have in each parish a convenient church built either of timber, brick, or stone, and decently adorned with everything necessary for the celebration of divine service.

If a parish be of greater extent than ordinary, it hath generally a chapel of ease, and some of the parishes have two such chapels besides the church for the greater convenience of the parishioners. In these chapels the minister preaches alternately, always leaving a reader to read prayers and homily when he can't attend himself.

The people are generally of the Church of England, which is the religion established by law in that country, from which there are very few dissenters. Yet liberty of conscience is given to all other congregations pretending to Christianity on condition they submit to all parish duties. They have no more than five conventicles amongst them, namely, three small meetings of Quakers and two of Presbyterians. 'Tis observed that those counties where the Presbyterian meetings are produce very mean tobacco and for that reason can't get an orthodox minister to stay amongst them, but whenever they could the people very orderly went to church. As for the Quakers, 'tis observed by letting them alone they decrease daily.

The maintenance for a minister there is appointed by law at sixteen thousand pounds of tobacco per annum (be the parish great or small) as also a dwelling house and glebe, together with certain perquisites for marriages and funeral sermons. That which makes the difference in the benefices of the clergy is the value of the tobacco according to the distinct species of it or according to the place of its growth. Besides, in large and rich parishes more marriages will probably happen and more funeral sermons.

The fee by law for a funeral sermon is forty shillings or four hundred pounds of tobacco; for a marriage by license twenty shillings or two hundred pounds of tobacco, and where the banns are proclaimed only five shillings or fifty pounds of tobacco.

When these salaries were granted the Assembly valued tobacco at ten shillings per hundred, at which rate the sixteen thousand pounds comes to forscore pounds sterling. But in all parishes where the sweet-scented grows it has generally been sold of late for near double that value and never under.

In some parishes likewise there are stocks of cattle and Negroes on the glebes which are also allowed to the minister for his use and encouragement, he only being accountable for the surrender of the same value when he leaves the parish.

Probates of wills and administrations are according to their law grantable by the county courts, but the commission must be signed by the governor without fee. Marriage licenses are issued by the clerks of those courts and signed by the first justice in commission or by any other person deputed by the governor, for which a fee of twenty shillings must be paid to the governor. The power of induction upon presentation of ministers is also by their law lodged in the governor's hands. All which acts are contained in the first revisal of their laws, since which her Majesty and her royal predecessors have always been pleased to give an instruction to their governors to that purpose.

In the year 1642, when the sectaries began to spread themselves so much in England, the Assembly made a law against them to prevent their preaching and propagating their doctrines in that colony. They admitted none to preach in their churches but ministers ordained by some reverend bishop of the Church of England; and the governor for the time being, as the most suitable public person among them, was left sole judge of the certificates of such ordination, and so he has continued ever since.

The only thing I have heard the clergy complain of there is what they call precariousness in their livings. That is, they have not inductions generally and therefore are not entitled to a freehold, but are liable without trial or crime alleged to to be put out by the vestry. And though some have prevailed with their vestries to present them for induction, yet the greater number of the ministers have no induction but are entertained from year to year or for term of years by agreement with their vestries. Yet are they very rarely turned out without some great provocation, and then if they have not been abominably scandalous they immediately get other parishes. For there is no benefice whatsoever in that country that remains without a parson if they can get one, and no qualified minister ever yet returned from that country for want of preferment. They have now about a dozen vacant parishes.

For the well-governing of these and all other parochial affairs, a vestry is appointed in each parish. These vestries consist of twelve gentlemen of the parish and were first chosen by the vote of the parishioners, but upon the death of one have been continued by the survivors electing another in his place. These are the patrons of the church, and in the name of the parish have the presentation of ministers as well as the sole power of all parish assessments. They are qualified for this employment by subscribing to be conformable to the doctrine and discipline of the Church of England. If there be a minister incumbent, he is always chief of the vestry.

For the ease of the vestry in general and for discharging the business of the parish, they choose two from among themselves to be church wardens, which must be annually changed, that the burden may lie equally upon all. The business of these church wardens is to see the orders and agreements of the vestry performed, to collect all the parish tobaccos and distribute them to the several claimants, to make up the accounts of the parish, and to present all profaneness and immorality.

By these the tobacco of the minister is collected and brought home to him in hogsheads convenient for shipping so that he is at no further trouble but to receive it in that condition. This was ordained by the law of the country for the ease of the ministers that so they being delivered from the trouble of gathering in their dues may have the more time to apply themselves to the exercises of their holy function and live in a decency suitable to their order. It may here be observed that the labor of a dozen Negroes does but answer this salary and seldom yields a greater crop of sweet-scented tobacco than is allowed to each of their ministers.

The established religion is that of the church of England; and there are very few Dissenters of any denomination in this province. There are at present between sixty and seventy clergymen; men in general of sober and exemplary lives. They have each a glebe of two or three hundred acres of land, a house, and a salary established by law of 16,000 weight of tobacco, with an allowance of 1700 more for shrinkage. This is delivered to them in hogsheads ready packed for exportation, at the most convenient warehouse. The presentation of livings is in the hands of the vestry; which is a standing body of twelve members, invested with the sole power of raising levies, settling the repairs of the church, and regulating other parochial business. They were originally elected by the people of the several parishes; but now fill up vacancies themselves. If the vestry does not present to a living in less than twelve months, it lapses to the governor. The diocesan is the bishop of London; who has a power of appointing a commissary to preside over, and convene the clergy on particular occasions; and to censure, or even suspend them, in cases of neglect or immorality. His salary is 100 l. sterling per annum; and he is generally of the council, which is of equal emolument to him.*

---

* The commissary is commonly president of the college, and has the parish of Williamsburg, or some other lucrative parish, which render him about 350 l. a year: so that his annual income is between 5 and 600 l.

An unhappy disagreement has lately arisen between the clergy and the laity, which, it is to be feared, may be of serious consequence. The cause of it was this. Tobacco being extremely scarce from a general failure of the crop, the assembly passed an act to oblige the clergy and all public officers to receive their stipends in money instead of tobacco. This the clergy remonstrated against, alledging the hardship of being obliged to take a small price for their tobacco, when it bore an extravagant one; seeing they never had any kind of compensation allowed, when it was so plentiful as to be almost a drug. They sent over an agent to England, and the law was repealed. This greatly exasperated the people; and such is their mutual animosity at this time, that, I fear, it will not easily subside, or be forgotten.

With regard to the law in question, it was certainly a very hard one; and I doubt whether, upon principles of free government, it can be justified; or whether the assembly can legally interpose any farther, than, in cases of necessity, to oblige the clergy to receive their salaries in money instead of tobacco, at the current price of tobacco. They may, I am persuaded, in cases of exigency, always make, and might then have made, such a law, without any considerable detriment to the colony: for, supposing the price of tobacco to be, what it was at that time, about fifty shillings currency per hundred, what would the whole sum be, were the clergy to be paid ad valorem? Not 20,000 l. sterling. There are in Virginia, as I observed before, about sixty-five clergymen: each of these is allowed 16,000 weight of tobacco; which, at the rate of fifty shillings currency per hundred, amounts to 400 l.; 400 l. multiplied by 65, is equal to 26,000 l.; which, allowing 40 per cent. discount, the difference of exchange, is about 18,571 l. sterling. Now what is this sum to such a colony as Virginia? But to this it will be said, perhaps, why should the clergy be gainers in a time of public distress, when every one else is a sufferer? The clergy will doubtless reply, and why should the clergy be the only sufferers in plentiful seasons, when all but themselves are gainers? Upon the whole, however, as on the one hand I disapprove of the proceedings of the assembly in this affair; so, on the other, I cannot approve of the steps which were taken by the clergy: that violence of temper; that disrespectful behaviour towards the governor; that unworthy treatment of their commissary; and, to mention nothing else, that confusion of proceeding in the convention, of which some, though not the majority, as has been invidiously represented, were guilty; these things were surely unbecoming the sacred character they are invested with; and the moderation of those persons, who ought in all things to imitate the conduct of their divine Master. If, instead of flying out in invectives against the legislature; or accusing the governor of having given up the cause of religion by passing the bill; when, in fact, had he rejected it, he would never have been able to have got any supplies during the course of the war, though ever so much wanted; if, instead of charging the commissary with want of zeal for having exhorted them to moderate measures, they had followed the prudent counsels of that excellent man, and had acted with more temper and moderation, they might, I am persuaded, in a very short time, have obtained any redress they could reasonably have desired. The people in general were extremely well affected towards the clergy, and had expressed their regard for them in several instances; they were sensible, moreover, that their salaries were too scanty to support them with dignity, and there had been some talk about raising them: had the clergy therefore, before they applied to England, only offered a memorial to the assembly, setting forth that they thought the act extremely hard upon them, as their salaries were small; and that they hoped the assembly would take their case into consideration, and enable them to live with that decency which became their character; I am persuaded, from the knowledge which I have of the people in general, and from repeated conversations with several members of the assembly, that they might have obtained almost any thing they could have wished; if not, they undoubtedly would have had reason to appeal. But, instead of this, without applying to the assembly for relief, after the act was passed, (for before, indeed, some of them did apply to the speaker in private) they flew out into the most violent invectives, immediately sent over an agent to England, and appealed to his majesty in council. The result has been already related.

The colonial South has often been contrasted with Puritan new England, but in many ways—since they grew from the same stock—they were remarkably similar. One common heritage they shared was a belief in witchcraft—the ability to perform acts supernaturally. In the 17th century witches—white and black—were identified by certain marks or unnatural signs on the body; often they were just plain ugly. The following excerpts are from the trial of

Grace Sherwood, an accused witch, in Princess Anne County, Virginia, in 1705, some years after the more famous Salem trials. The complete trial is printed in the Collections of the Virginia Historical and Philosophical Society, *vol. 1 (1833), pp. 73-78.*

At a Court held the 7th March 1705/6 [names of 9 justices]
Whereas a complaint have been to this Court by Luke Hill & his wife that one Grace Sherwood of the County was and have been a long time suspected of witchcraft & have been as such represented wherefore the Sherrif at the last court was ordered to summon a Jury of women to the Court to serch her on the said suspicion, she assenting to the same—and after the Jury was impannelled and sworn & sent out to make due inquirery & inspection into all cercumstances after a mature consideration they bring in their verdict; we of the Jury have serc[h]ath Grace Sherwood & have found two things like titts with severall other spots—[names of 12 women]

At a Court held the 2nd May 1706 [5 justices present]
Whereas a former Complaint was brought against Grace Sherwood for suspicion of Witchcraft, which by the attorny General's report to his Excellency in Council was too Generall & not charging her with any perticular act, therefore represented to them that Princess Ann Court might if they thought fitt have her examined de novo [again] & the Court being of opinion that there is great cause of suspicion doe therefore order that the Sherrif take the said Grace into his safe costody untill she shall give bond & security for her appearance at the next Court to be examined De novo & that the Constable of that presinkt goe with the Sherrif & serch the said Graces house & all suspicious places carfully for all Images & such like things as may any way strengthen the suspicion & it is likewise ordered that the Sherrif summon an able Jury of women also all evidences as cann give in any thing against her in evidence in behalf of our Sovereign Lady the Qeen to attend the next Court accordingly. . . .

At a Court held the 7th of June 1706 [6 justices]
Whereas at the last Court an order was past that the Sherrif should sommons an able Jury of women to serch Grace Sherrwood on suspicion of witchcraft which although the same was performed by the Sherrif yet they refused, and did not appear; it is therefore Ordered that the same persons be again sommoned to appear next Court to serch her on the aforesaid suspicion & that He likewise sommon all evidences that he shall be informed of as materiall in the Complaint &

that She continue in the Sherrif's Costody unless she give good bond and security for her appearance at the next Court and that she be of good behaviour towards her Majesty & all her leidge people in the meantime.

At a Court held the 5th July Anno Domine 1706 [4 justices]

Whereas for this severall Courts the bussiness between Luke Hill & Grace Sherwood on suspicion of Witchcraft have been for severall things omitted particularly for want of a Jury to serch her & the Court being doubtfull that they should not get one, this Court & being willing to have all means possible tryed either to acquit her or to give more strength to the suspicion that she might be dealt with as deserved, therefore It was Ordered that this day by her own consent to be tryed in the water by ducking, but the weather being very rainy & bad soe that possibly it might endanger her health, it is therefore ordered that the Sherrif request the Justices . . . to appear on Wednesday next by tenn of the Clock at the Court-house & that he secure the body of the said Grace till the time to be forthcoming then to be dealt with as aforesaid.

At a Court held the 10th July 1706 [7 justices]

Whereas Grace Sherrwood being suspected of Witchcraft have a long time waited for a fit opportunity for a further examination & by her consent & approbation of the Court it is ordered that the Sherrif take all such convenient assistance of boats & men as shall be by him thought fit to meet at Jonathan Harper's plantation in order to take the said Grace forwith & but [dunk] her into above man's depth & try her how she swims therein, alwayes having care of her life to preserve her from drowning & as soon as she comes out that he request as many antient & knowing women as possible he cann to serch her carefully for all teats, Spotts & marks about her body not usuall on others & that as they find the same to make report on oath to the truth thereof to the Court & further it is ordered that some women be requested to shift & serch her before she goe into the water that she carry nothing about her to cause any further serspicion.

Whereas on complaint of Luke Hill in behalf of her Magesty that now is against Grace Sherrwood for a person suspected of witchcraft & having had sundry evidences sworne against her proving many cercumstances & which she did not make any excuse or little or nothing to say in her own behalf only seemed to rely on what the Court should doe & therefore consent to be tryed in the water & likewise to be serched again, which experiments being tryed & she swiming

When therein & bound contrary to custom & the Judgements of all the spectators & afterwards being serched by five antient women who have declared on oath that she is not like them nor noe other woman that they knew of, having two things like titts on her private parts of a Black coller being blacker than the rest of her body, all which cercumstance the Court weighing in their consideration doe therefore order that the Sherrif take the said Grace into his costody & to comit her body to the common Joal of this County, their to secure her by irons or otherwise there to remain till such time as he shall be otherwise directed in order for her coming to the common goal of the Countey to be brought to a future tryall there.

Outside Virginia the simplicities of religious life vanished, especially for Anglican missionaries trying to bring the backcountry folk into the Church of England. Rev. John Blair went out in 1704 and Charles Woodmason followed in 1766. The religious conditions they witnessed are described in Narratives of Early Carolina, 1650-1708, *ed. Alexander S. Salley, Jr. (New York, 1911), pp. 214-218, and* The Carolina Backcountry on the Eve of the Revolution, *ed. Richard J. Hooker (Chapel Hill, 1953), pp. 76-81 (notes, possibly for the Bishop of London), 95-104 (sermon against the Baptists and Presbyterians).*

I was ordained, in order to go to the plantations, 12th April, 1703, and then received the queen's bounty of £ 20, and, soon after, my Lord Weymouth's bounty of £ 50; upon which I lived in England till the 1st of October following, which, together with my fitting out for such a voyage and country, consumed the most part of my money. I had likewise £ 5 sent me by my lord of London to Portsmouth, and when I landed in Virginia I had no more than £ 25.

I landed in Virginia, 14th of January, 1704; and, as soon as I could conveniently travel, I waited upon the governor, and immediately after made the best of my way into the country where I was bound.

I arrived amongst the inhabitants, after a tedious and troublesome journey, 24th *ditto*. I was then obliged to buy a couple of horses, which cost me fourteen pounds,—one of which was for a guide, because there is no possibility for a stranger to find his road in that country, for if he once goes astray (it being such a desert country) it is a great hazard if he ever finds his road again. Beside, there are mighty inconveniences in travelling there, for the roads are not only deep and difficult to be found, but there are likewise seven great rivers in the country, over which there is no passing of horses, except two of them, one of which the Quakers have settled a ferry over for their own conveniency, and nobody but themselves have the privilege of it; so that at the passing over the rivers, I was obliged either to borrow or hire horses, which was both troublesome and chargeable, insomuch that in little more than two months I was obliged to dispose of the necessaries I carried over for my own use, to satisfy my creditors.

I found in the country a great many children to be baptized, where I baptized about a hundred; and there are a great many still to be baptized, whose parents would not condescend to have them baptized with god-fathers and god-mothers.

I married none in the country, for that was a perquisite belonging to the magistrates, which I was not desirous to deprive them of.

I preached twice every Sunday, and often on the week-days, when their vestries met, or could appoint them to bring their children to be baptized.

I called a vestry in each precinct, in my first progress through the country, to whom I gave an account of my Lord Weymouth's charitable bounty in supporting my mission among them, and likewise of the good designs the honorable society had for them, as I was informed by Mr. Amy that they had settled £ 50 per annum for the maintenance of two clergymen amongst them; and likewise a proposal that Dr. Bray desired me to make to them, that, upon their procuring good glebes, he doubted not that there might be a settlement made for the advantage of the Church, such as there is in the island of Bermudas, *viz.*, two slaves and a small stock in each precinct, and that to be continued good by the incumbent to his successor, which will be a lasting estate to the Church.

They have built in the country three small churches, and have three glebes.

In the three chief precincts, there is a reader established in each, to whom they allow a small salary, who reads morning and evening prayer every Lord's day, with two sermons, and I took care to furnish them with books from the library before I came away.

I remained very well satisfied in the country till their Assembly sat, which was on 1st March, where I expected they would propose a settlement for my maintenance; and they taking no care of it, together with my then circumstances, which were but very indifferent, discouraged me very much, and occasioned my first thoughts of returning to England; for I was informed before I went thither that there was £ 30 per annum, settled by law, to be paid in each precinct for the maintenance of a minister, which law was sent over hither to be confirmed by their lords proprietors, and it being supposed not to be a competency for a minister to live on, was sent back again without confirmation, whereof the Quakers took the advantage, and will endeavor to prevent any such law passing for the future, for they are the greatest number in the Assembly, and are unanimous, and stand truly to one another in whatsoever may be to their interest. For the country may be divided into four sorts of people: first, the Quakers, who are the most powerful enemies to Church government, but a people very ignorant of what they profess. The second sort are a great many who have no religion, but would be Quakers, if by that they were not obliged to lead a more moral life than they are willing to comply to. A third sort are something like Presbyterians, which sort is upheld by some idle fellows who have left their lawful employment, and preach and baptize through the country, without any manner of orders from any sect or pretended Church. A fourth sort, who are really zealous for the interest of the Church, are the fewest in number, but the better sort of people, and would do very much for the settlement of the Church government there, if not opposed by these three precedent sects; and although they be all three of different pretensions, yet they all concur together in one common cause to prevent any thing that will be chargeable to them, as they allege Church government will be, if once established by law. And another great discouragement these poor people have, is a governor who does not in the least countenance them in this business, but rather discourages them.

Finding it impossible to travel through the country at that rate I began, I was resolved to settle in one precinct, but the people, all alleging that my Lord Weymouth's charity was universally designed for the whole country, would not consent to it; which bred some disturbance amongst them, upon which I was advised, by some of the best friends of the Church, to come over and represent their condition to the honorable society, not only of their want of ministers but likewise of inhabitants to maintain them; and their desires, they complying with my necessities, was a powerful argument, considering I was then reduced to my last stake, and knew not where, or upon what account, to be further supplied. Besides, such a solitary, toilsome, and hard living as I met with there were very sufficient discouragements. I was distant from any minister one hundred and twenty miles, so that if any case of difficulty or doubt should happen, with whom should I consult? And for my travelling through the country, I rode one day with another, Sundays only excepted, about thirty miles *per diem* in the worst roads that ever I saw; and have sometimes lain whole nights in the woods.

I will now endeavor to show you how inefficient a single man's labors would be amongst so scattered a people. In the first place, suppose him minister of one precinct (whereas there are five in the country), and this precinct, as they are all bounded with two rivers, and those rivers at least twenty miles distant, without any inhabitants on the road, for they plant only on the rivers, and they are planted at length upon those rivers at least twenty miles, and to give all those inhabitants an opportunity of hearing a sermon, or bringing their children to be baptized, which must be on the Sabbath, for they won't spare time of another day, and must be in every ten miles distant, for five miles is the furthest they will bring their children, or willingly come themselves; so that he must, to do his duty effectually, be ten or twelve weeks in making his progress through one precinct.

You may also consider the distance that the new colony of Pamtico is from the rest of the inhabitants of the country, for any man that has tried it would sooner undertake a voyage from this city to Holland than that, for beside a pond of five miles broad, and nothing to carry one over but a small perryauger, there are about fifty miles desert to pass through, without any human creature inhabiting in it. I think it likewise reasonable to give you an account of a great nation of Indians that live in that government, computed to be no less than 100,000, many of which live amongst the English, and all, as I can understand, a very civilized people.

I have often conversed with them, and have been frequently in their towns: those that can speak English among them seem to be very willing and fond of being Christians, and in my opinion there might be methods taken to bring over a great many of them. If there were no hopes of making them Christians, the advantage of having missionaries among them would redound to the advantage of the government, for if they should once be brought over to a French interest (as we have too much reason to believe there are some promoters amongst them for that end by their late actions), it would be, if not to the utter ruin, to the great prejudice of all the English plantations on the continent of America.

I have here in brief set down what I have to say, and shall be ready to answer to any questions the honorable society shall think convenient to ask me concerning the country; and shall be both ready and willing to serve them anywhere upon such encouragement as I can live, according to my education, after my Lord Weymouth ceases to lay his commands on me.

I have made a considerable losing voyage of it this time, both by my troublesome travelling in America, and likewise by being taken into France, where I was a prisoner of war nine weeks, and was forced to make use of my credit for my sustenance; and have lived in the same circumstances since I came to England, without any manner of relief, which has been very troublesome to me, all of which has brought me considerably in debt, near £35, and now in no way to pay it, without my charitable benefactor or the honorable society judge my labors worthy a reward.

As to North Carolina, the State of Religion therein, is greatly to be lamented—If it can be said, That there is any Religion, or a Religious Person in it. A Church was founded at Wilmington in 1753. Another at Brunswick in 1756, the Walls of each are carried up about 10 or 12 feet and so remain. Governour Dobbs us'd Great Endeavours to get these Buildings finish'd, and to lay out Parishes—But lived not to effect it—But the present Governour has got an Act pass'd, for a Church to be built in each Parish or Distric, and Church Matters to be settled on the Plan of South Carolina. He has given Public Notice hereof to the Clergy—Inviting of them to come abroad Promising of them his Protection Encouragement and Support: At the same time mentioning what Numbers of Sectaries overspread the Country, and the Danger that not only the Church Established, but even Religion it Self will be totally lost and destroyed if not quickly attended too.

Here is an opening—A large Harvest for all that are sincerely dispos'd to act for the Glory of God and the Good of Souls—How many thousands who never saw, much less read, or ever heard a Chapter of the Bible! How many Ten thousands who never were baptized or heard a Sermon! And thrice Ten thousand, who never heard of the Name of Christ, save in Curses and Execrations! Lamentable!

Lamentable is the Situation of these People, as to Spirituals, Even beyond the Power of Words to describe.

There are 2 or 3 Itinerant Ministers in the Northern Part (or Lord Granvills Division) of the Province, and several Small Chapels are built in that Distric—But not a Church or Minister in any one Town of their Province, Maritime or Inland.

In the Back Part of this Country between the Heads of Pedee and Cape Fear Rivers, is a Distric of 12000 Acres, formerly granted to Whitfield, and by Him sold to Count Zinzendorff—It is very rich Land—scituated just at foot of the lower Hills, and where the Springs take their Rise, that form these Great Rivers above mentioned. The Spot is not only Rich, fertile, and luxuriant, but the most Romantic in Nature Sir Philip Sidneys Description of Arcadia, falls short of this *real* Arcadia Georgia, Circassia, Armenia, or whatever Region it may be compared too. To this Spot Zinzindorff transplanted his Hernhutters; who being join'd by others from Pensylvania, and Elsewhere now form a very large and numerous Body of People, Acting under their own Laws and Ordinances, independent of the Community, Constitution or Legislature in and over them. They are a Set of *Recabites* among the People of *Israel*—Forming a Distinc[t] Body, different in all things from All People. Here they have laid out two Towns—*Bethelem* and *Bethsada*; delightfully charming! Rocks, Cascades, Hills, Vales, Groves, Plains—Woods.

The most zealous among the Sects, to propagate their Notions, and form Establishments, are the Anabaptists. When the Church of England was established in Carolina, the Presbyterians made Great Struggles; but finding themselves too weak, they determin'd to effect that by Cunning (the Principles they work by, for they are all Moles) which Strength could not effect. Wherefore, as Parish Churches were built only along the Sea Coast, they built a Sett of Meeting Houses quite back behind in the Interior Parts—Imitating the French—who by making a Chain of Forts from Canada to Louisiana endeavour'd to circumscribe the English, and prevent the Extension of their Trade. So did the Presbyterians with our Church—If they could not *suppress*, they would *cramp* the Progress of the Liturgy and Church Establish'd. And accordingly did, erect Meeting Houses as before said. None of the Church oppos'd Them—And the Almighty (by taking these People in their own Craft) have suffer'd them to fall into the

Nett they spread for others. For, the Anabaptists in Pensylvania, resolving themselves into a Body, and determined to settle their Principles in ev[e]ry vacant Quarter, began to establish Meeting Houses also on the Borders—And by their Address and Assiduity, have worm'd the Presbyterians out of all these their strong Holds, and drove them away—So that the Baptists are now the most numerous and formidable Body of People which the Church has to encounter with, in the Interior and Back Parts of the Province And the Antipathy that these two Sects bear each other, is astonishing. Wherefore, a Presbyterian would sooner marry ten of his Children to Members of the Church of England than one to a Baptist. The same from the Baptists as to the Presbyterians—Their Rancour is surprizing—But the Church reaps great Good by it—And thro' their Jealousies, gains Ground on them very fast.

But these Baptists have great Prevalence and footing in North Carolina, and have taken such deep Root there that it will require long Time and Pains to grub up their Layers.

The Manners of the North Carolinians in General, are Vile and Corrupt—The whole Country is a Stage of Debauchery Dissoluteness and Corruption—And how can it be otherwise? The People are compos'd of the Out Casts of all the other Colonies who take Refuge there. The Civil Police is hardly yet establish'd. But they are so numerous—The Necessaries of Life are so cheap, and so easily acquir'd, and propagation being unrestricted, that the Encrease of People there, is inconceivable, even to themselves.

Marriages (thro' want of Clergy) are perform'd by ev'ry ordinary Magistrate. Polygamy is very Common—Celibacy much more—Bastardy, no Disrepute—Concubinage General—When will this *Augean* Stable be cleans'd!

But surely, if Persons have received more and better Edification by resorting to the Schism Shop, then by continuing constant in Well doing at their own Chapel certainly it will display it Self in their Lives and Manners. This is the Test by which We must try the Validity of these Assertions—And therefore I hope it will not be thought invidious if I enter into a few Particulars. Because I hear so much Talk about *Conversion*, certainly there must be some very Great Reformation of Morals among You: But I would not have Te Deum sung before the Victory be gain'd.

And as for Hymns We do not disallow of them, provided they be Solemn, Sublime, Elegant and Devout—Fit to be offer'd up to the Throne of Grace—And such can be furnish'd to any Religious Society, desirous of them.

The best Things are most liable to Abuse—And these Singing Matches lie under the Imputation of being only Rendezvous of Idlers, under the Mask of Devotion. Meetings for Young Persons to carry on Intrigues and Amours. For all Classes of Villains, and the Vicious of both Sexes to make Assignations; and for others to indulge themselves in Acts of Intemperance and Wantoness, So that these Religious Societies are Evil spoken off, and therefore ought to be abolished conformable to what was done in the Primitive Times. The first Christians us'd to assemble at Nights, at the Tombs of the Martyrs, and there sing Hymns and perform Prayers. But as this gave Offence to the Heathens, and occasion'd the whole Body to be censur'd for the Irregularities of a Few it was judged proper to abolish these Nocturnal Meetings: And this Act of the Primitive Church ought to be a Rule to us at present: For it is rather better to decline an Innocent Duty that may be productive of some Good, rather than to have it perverted by base Minds to many Purposes of Evil:

But let us go on, and examine if in the General Corruption of Manners these New Lights have made any Reform in the Vice of Drunkenness? Truly, I wot not. There is not one Hogshead of Liquor less consum'd since their visiting us, or any Tavern shut up—So far from it, that there has been Great Increase of Both. Go to any Common Muster or Vendue, Will you not see the same Fighting, Brawling Gouging, Quarreling as ever? And this too among the Holy ones of our New Israel? Are Riots, Frolics, Races, Games, Cards, Dice, Dances, less frequent now than formerly? Are fewer persons to be seen in Taverns? or reeling or drunk on the Roads? And have any of the Godly Storekeepers given up their Licences, or refus'd to retail Poison? If this can be made appear, I will yield the Point. But if [it] can be made apparent that a much greater Quantity of Rum is now expended in private families than heretofore—That the greater Part of these religious Assemblies are calculated for private Entertainments, where each brings his Quota and which often terminates in Intemperance and Intoxication of both Sexes, Young and Old: That one half of those who resort to these Assemblies Go more for sake of Liquor, than Instruction, or Devotion. That if it be proven that Liquor has been top'd about even in their very Meeting Houses, and the

Preachers refreshed with Good Things, and after the Farce ended Stuff'd and Cramm'd almost to bursting, then it must be granted that little or no Reform has been made among the Vulgar in Point of Intemperance save only among some few Persons in some Places where the Mode only is chang'd, and drinking in Public wav'd for the Indulgence of double the Consumption in Private.

The horrid Vice of Swearing has long been a reproach to the Back Inhabitants, and very justly—for few Countries on Earth can equal these Parts as to this greivous Sin. But has it ceas'd since the Admission of rambling Fanatics among us? I grant that it has with and among many, whom they have gain'd to their Sect. Yet still it too much prevails. But the Enormity of this Vice, when at the Highest, produc'd no Evils, Jarrs, disturbances Strifes, Contentions, Variance, Dissimulations, Envyings, Slanders, Backbitings and a thousand other Evils that now disturb both the Public Places and repose of Individuals. So that where they have cast out one Devil, Seven, and twice Seven others have enter'd In and possess the Man. For never was so much Lying, Calumny, Defamation, and all hellish Evils and vexations of this Sort that can spring from the Devil and his Angels, so brief so prevalent, so abounding as since the Arrival of these villanous Teachers, Who blast, blacken, Ruin, and destroy the Characters, Reputations, Credit and Fame of all Persons not linked with them to the Ruin of Society, the Peace of families, and the Settlement of the Country.

We will further enquire, if Lascivousness, or Wantoness, Adultery or Fornication [are] less common than formerly, before the Arrival of these *Holy* Persons? Are there fewer Bastards born? Are more Girls with their Virginity about them, Married, than were heretofore? The Parish Register will prove the Contrary: There are rather more Bastards, more Mullatoes born than before. Nor out of 100 Young Women that I marry in a Year have I seen, or is there seen, Six but what are with Child? And this as Common with the Germans on other Side the River, as among You on this Side: So that a Minister is accounted as a Scandalous Person for even coming here to marry such People, and for baptizing their Bastard Children as the Law obliges Me to register All Parties who are Married, and all Children Born. This occasions such Numbers (especially of the Saints) to fly into the next Province, and up to the German Ministers and any where to get Married, to prevent their being register'd, as therefrom the Birth of their Children would be trac'd: And as for Adulteries, the present State of most Persons around 9/10 of whom now labour under a filthy Distemper (as is well known to all) puts that Matter out of all Dispute and shews that the Saints however outwardly Precise and Reserved are not one Whit more Chaste than formerly, and possibly are more privately Vicious.

And nothing more leads to this Than what they call their Love Feasts and Kiss of Charity. To which Feasts, celebrated at Night, much Liquor is privately carried, and deposited on the Roads, and in Bye Paths and Places. The Assignations made on Sundays at the Singing Clubs, are here realized. And it is no wonder that Things are as they are, when many Young Persons have 3. 4. 5. 6 Miles to walk home in the dark Night, with Convoy, thro' the Woods? Or staying perhaps all Night at some Cabbin (as on Sunday Nights) and sleeping together either doubly or promiscuously? Or a Girl being mounted behind a Person to be carried home, or any wheres. All this indeed contributes to multiply Subjects for the King in this frontier Country, and so is wink'd at by the Magistracy and Parochial Officers but at same time, gives great Occasion to the Enemies of Virtue, to triumph, for Religion to be scandalized and brought into Contempt; For all Devotion to be Ridicul'd, and in the Sequel, will prove the Entire banishment and End of all Religion—Confusion—Anarchy and ev'ry Evil Work will be the Consequence of such Lewdness and Immorality.

But certainly these Reformers have put some Stop to the many Thefts and Depradations so openly committed of late Years?—To answer this Question recourse must be had to the Magistrates and Courts of Justice, who are ready to declare, that since the Appearance of these New Lights, more Enormities of all Kinds have been committed—More Robberies, Thefts, Murders, Plunderings, Burglaries and Villanies of ev'ry Kind, than ever before. And the Reason hereof, Is, That most of these Preaching fellows were most notorious Theives, Jockeys, Gamblers, and what not in the Northern Provinces, and since their Reception and Success here have drawn Crowds of their old Acquaintances after them; So that the Country never was so full as at present of Gamesters, Prostitutes, Filchers, Racers, Fidlers and all the refuse of Mankind. All which follow these Teachers, and under the Mask of Religion carry on many detestable Practises. In short, they have filled the Country with Idle and Vagrant Persons, who live by their Criminalities. For it is a Maxim with these Vermin of Religion, That a Person must first be a Sinner e're He can be a Saint. And I am bold to say, That the Commonality around, do not now make half the Crops nor are 1/4 so Industrious, as 3 Years ago. Because half their Time is wasted in traveling about to this and that Lecture—and to hear this and that fine Man, So that they are often a Month absent from their families. . . .

For only draw a Comparison between them and Us, and let an Impartial Judge determine where *Offence* may cheifly be taken, At our Solemn, Grave, and Serious Sett Forms, or their Wild Extempore Jargon, nauseaus to any Chaste or refin'd Ear. There are so many Absurdities committed by them, as wou'd shock one of our *Cherokee* Savages; And was a Sensible Turk or Indian to view some of their Extravagancies it would quickly determine them against Christianity. Had any such been in their Assembly as last Sunday when they communicated, the Honest Heathens would have imagin'd themselves rather amidst a Gang of frantic Lunatics broke out of Bedlam, rather than among a Society of religious Christians, met to celebrate the most sacred and Solemn Ordinance of their Religion. Here, one Fellow mounted on a Bench with the Bread, and bawling, *See the Body of Christ*, Another with the Cup running around, and bellowing—*Who cleanses his Soul with the Blood of Christ*, and a thousand other Extravagancies—One on his knees in a Posture of Prayer—Others singing—some howling—These Ranting—Those Crying—Others dancing, Skipping, Laughing and rejoycing. Here two or 3 Women falling on their Backs, kicking up their Heels, exposing their Nakedness to all Bystanders and others sitting Pensive, in deep Melancholy lost in Abstraction, like Statues, quite insensible—and when rous'd by the Spectators from their pretended Reveries Transports, and indecent Postures and Actions declaring they knew nought of the Matter. That their Souls had taken flight to Heav'n, and they knew nothing of what they said or did. Spect[at]ors were highly shocked at such vile Abuse of sacred Ordinances! And indeed such a Scene was sufficient to make the vilest Sinner shudder. Their Teacher, so far from condemning, or reproving, them, call'd it, the Work of God, and returned Thanks for Actions deserving of the Pillory and Whipping Post. But that would not have been *New* to some of them. And if they can thus transgress all bounds of Decency Modesty, and Morality, in such an Open Public Manner, it is not hard to conceive what may pass at their Nocturnal Meetings, and Private Assemblies. Is there any thing like this in the Church of England to give Offence?

But another vile Matter that does and must give Offence to all Sober Minds Is, what they call their *Experiences*; It seems, that before a Person be dipp'd, He must give an Account of his Secret Calls, Conviction, Conversion, Repentance &c &c. Some of these Experiences have been so ludicrous and ridiculous that *Democritus* in Spite of himself must have burst with Laughter. Others, altogether as blasphemous Such as their Visions, Dreams, Revelations—and the like; Too many, and too horrid to be mention'd. Nothing in the *Alcoran* Nothing that can be found in all the Miracles of the Church of Rome, and all the Reveries of her Saints can be so absurd, or so Enthusiastic, as what has gravely been recited in that *Tabernacle* Yonder—To the Scandal of Religion and Insult of Common Sense. And to heighten the Farce, To see two or three fellows with fix'd Countenances and grave Looks, hearing all this Nonsense for Hours together, and making particular Enquiries, when, How, Where, in what Manner, these Miraculous Events happen'd—To see, I say, a Sett of Mongrels under Pretext of Religion, Sit, and hear for Hours together a String of Vile, cook'd up, Silly and Senseless Lyes, What they know to be Such, What they are Sensible has not the least foundation in Truth or Reason, and to encourage Persons in such Gross Inventions must grieve, must give great Offence to ev'ry one that has the Honour of Christianity at Heart.

Then again to see them Divide and Sub divide, Split into Parties—Rail at and excommunicate one another—Turn out of Meeting, and receive into another—And a Gang of them getting together and gabbling one after the other (and sometimes disputing against each other) on Abstruse Theological Question—Speculative Points—Abstracted Notions, and Scholastic Subtelties, such as the greatest Metaph[ys]icians and Learned Scholars never yet could define, or agree on—To hear Ignorant Wretches, who can not write—Who never read ten Pages in any Book, and can hardly read the Alphabett discussing such Knotty Points for the Edification of their Auditors, is a Scene so farcical, so highly humoursome as excels any Exhibition of Folly that has ever yet appear'd in the World, and consequently must give High offence to all Inteligent and rational Minds.

If any Thing offensive beyond all This to greive the Hearts and Minds of serious Christians presents it Self to view among them, it is their Mode of Baptism, to which Lascivous Persons of both Sexes resort, as to a Public Bath. I know not whether it would not be less offensive to Modesty for them to strip wholly into Buff at once, than to be dipp'd with those very thin Linen Drawers they are equipp'd in—Which when wet, so closely adheres to the Limbs, as exposes the Nudities equally as if none at All. If this be not Offensive and a greivous Insult on all Modesty and Decency among Civiliz'd People I know not what can be term'd so. Certainly a few chosen Witnesses of the Sex of the Party, and performance of the Ceremony in a Tent, or Cover'd Place, would be equally as *Edifying*, as Persons being stript and their Privities expos'd before a gaping Multitude who resort to these Big Meetings (as they are term'd) as they would to a Bear or Bullbaiting.

It must give Great Scandal and Offence to all Serious Minds thus to see the Solemn Ordinances of God become the Sport, Pastime and Derision of Men—and to view them marching in Procession singing Hymns before the poor wet half naked Creature—Very edifying this! Just as much as I saw lately practis'd at Marriage of one of their Notable She Saints around whom (the Ceremony ended) they march'd in Circles singing Hymns, and chanting Orisons, with a vast Parade of Prayer Thanks givings and Religious Foppery; Which had such marvellous Effect on the virtuous Devotee as to cause her to bring a Child in five Months after, as a Proof that their Prayers for her being fruitful was answer'd.

VI. DEATH

How as old age regarded in the South? Why? How would you describe the "southern way of dying"? What do the inventories of deceased persons reveal about the way they lived?

Death in the colonial South was as noticeable as the weather or crops but certainly no more so. Disease, hostile Indians, and even suicide took their toll as they did elsewhere in the American colonies. Colonel Landon Carter was witness to death and its approach in his Diary, *edited by Jack P. Greene (Charlottesville, 1965).*

1772: 2 September. Quite cool and blowing. Mr. Robt. Barwell, the Counsellor, came here yesterday with Colo. Tayloe and his Lady. He is an unhappy man yet awhile in his thoughts. A widower in his 52d year of Age, a Grandfather, both of his sons' and his daughters' Children; too young to continue single; and too old for any Lady but the aged to associate with. And as he has never been one given to much reading, he seems to have nothing to be able to pass away his lonely hours with. In this situation, at Present, he is unhappy in not being able to think of anything but a wife in which every man nowadays exhibits but an odd and foolish scene of life, and as he grows older he must be miserable; for without books or a desire to read how can the aged injoy themselves, when the Young even their children seem to despise them. It is a pity that old age which everybody covets and everybody who lives must come to should be so contemptible in the eyes of the world. I experience it and therefore feel it; but I thank God my limbs as yet serve me to ride out, and my eyes by the help of glasses serve me to read and dispise them in my turn, as in this their follies are more conspicuous than common. Some few there are who fancy they ought to behave otherwise, and do so in the main, but not amongst my really ungrateful children. But as I wish them no ill in whom I will say enough of such Melancholly reflections.

1775: 22 September. Poor John Purcell, my overseer, I hear is dead. I always expected so generally as well as universal a Set in for bilious disorders would occasion some deaths but did not expect it in so hail a young man; but Possibly this has been no good Circumstance in his illness. A month ago when his mouth broke out I had a difficulty to keep it from a cancer, and was told he had been subject to it many years. As soon as that discharge got well, I recommended a purge, but as he was very well he declined it. A month after he complained of bitterness in his stomach. I advised to wash his stomach with weak tartar water. He agreed to it and two days after asked for it. I ordered 3 grains to a quart of water but he would have 5 grains of Nassau and I did hear took it off in a Spoon. I asked about it; he denyed it but owned he did not drink much water. A month after this, having been well, he grew loaded again with bile and asked again another Vomit. I ordered then 3 grains expressly; he kept it 4 days and then was very ill. I sent Nassau to see him and he got drunk and this was his last illness. A wench of mine says she saw him work his first and second Vomit with Cold milk, at least a gallon at a time, and she told him it would kill him. It is rare, but it does sometimes happen that People Purposely kill themselves. Certainly this man did so.

In the distant settlements of the South burial was often as difficult to get as a marriage license or baptism—and for the same reasons. The County Court Records of Accomack-Northampton, Virginia, 1632-1640, *ed. Susie M. Ames (Washington, 1954), p. 54, contain the record of one attempt to solve the problem.*

A Vestry holden at Acchawmack this 20th day of May 1636.
Present mr. william cotton, minister, mr. william Stonne, mr. william Burdet, mr. John wilkins, mr. John Neale, mr. Stephen Charelton, mr. Henry Bagwell.

It is ordered by this Vestry that the clarke of this parish shall have the full allowance of one peeke of corne and tow pounds of tobacco of every tythable person to be paid with the ministers tyths.

It is agreed that for every person buried in the Church, shall be payd unto the church wardens 50 lbs. of tobacco for the use of the s[exton.]

Likewise it is agreed that the clarke shall for every gr[ave] have tenn pounds of tobacco, but for [   ]. . . . 15 lbs of tobacco.

Haveing taken into consideration the remote liveing of the [members] of this parrish from the church. It is agreed that all suc[h persons as live at] the old plantation from the land of mrs. Graves unto Magoty Bay the head of the said old plantaton creeke that they shall have ther[?] bodys to be buried one part of the land of william Blower where william Berriman liveth and likewise that they give notice unto the minister and provide convenient meanes for his coming ther to bury the dead which who soever shall refuse such decent and christianlike burial that then they are to stand to the censure of this vestry, Alsoe it is agreed that the clarke shall have notice of all such dead people [soe that] he may be able to make the graves reddy which if any shall refuse to give notice, yet he shall be liable to pay 10 lbs of tobacco and if upon notice given the said clarke shall refuse to come and make the graves that then the said clarke shall stand the censure of the vestry, complaint being m[ade.]

Since land, livestock, and tools were the farmer's essentials, he normally made provision in his will to pass them on to his family. The inventories of estates of small farmers and great are eloquent testimony to the way they spent their lives as well as the way they died. The following inventories are taken from the County Court Records of Accomack-Northampton, *p. 112;* Bases of the Plantation Society, *ed. Aubrey C. Land (New York, 1969), pp. 194-197 (Maryland Hall of Records, Annapolis); and* William Fitzhugh and His Chesapeake World 1676-1701, *ed. Richard Beale Davis (Chapel Hill, 1963), pp. 382-385 (Virginia Historical Society).*

[*Widdow Hayes her estate appraised*]. THE Estate of John Hayes deceased praised this 15th of May 1638 by Henry Bagwell and William Berriman as followeth

Imprimis 1 Iron pott and hookes of 2 gallons and 1/2	050
" one brasse skillett with a Frame	025
" one brasse kettle 5 gallons and more	080
" one brasse kettle 2 gallons ould	025
" one Iron pestle	010
" ould hookes and a patched hoe	006
" one Fryeinge panne	020
" 1 greate traye	015
" 1 Indyan Bowle, 1 wooden plater	008
" 1 ould bible, 1 ould booke	015
" 1 hamar 1 pair of sheeres, 1 brush	010
" 1 porringer 2 spoones, 1 ould salte	003
" 1 Boxe with lock and key, 1 ould boale	010
" 1 Earthen Bottle	003
" ould table Board	010
" ould blanketts	012
" 1 ould pillowe with Feathers and Beare, 1 sheete	020
" 1 ould Flock bedd	035
	357

A Just and True Inventory of the Goods and Chattels and Credits of the Estate of Thomas Collins Late of This County Deceased in Current Money of This Province of Maryland

	£	s.	d.
To 3 cows and yearlings at 35/0 each 2 cows and calfs at 30/0 each	8	5	0
To 1 old horse 4 and 1 yearlen colt 20/0	5	0	0
To 5 very old sows and some pigs at 30/0 10 small shots 20/0	2	10	0
To 136 lbs. of old derty feathers and rotten ticks at 6 d. per lb.	3	8	0
To 3 old broken steds 5/0 1 grinding stone 6 d.	0	5	6
To sum very old rag[g]ed bed cloths at 15/0	0	15	0

To 11-1/2 lbs. old pewter at 13 d. per lb. 18 lbs. very old pewter at 6 d. per lb.	1 1	8-1/2
To 22-1/2 lbs. of old broken pewter at 4 d. per lb.	0 7	6
To 74 lbs. very old pot iron at 9 d. per lb. old cow bell 5/0	1 3	6
To 5 old broken barrels 1/0 each 2 old brace candle sticks 3/0	0 8	0
To 1 pare of old small stillards 2/6 1 pare spoon moles 2/6	0 5	0
To small parcell broken tub and palls	0 7	6
To 10 lbs. derty wool at 9 d. per lb. 12 glass bottels 3/0 [and] 1 old hakel 1/0	0 11	6
To 1 old box iron at 6 d. 1 tap 1/0 1 gun 12/6	0 14	6
To split barral gun 2/6 [and] 1 old gun barral 2/0	0 4	6
To 40 lbs. old iron at 3 d. per lb. To small parcell old lumber 5/0	0 15	0
To 1 old croscut saw 2/6 1 old hansaw 2/6	0 5	0
To 1 old vise eaten out with rust 1/0 [and] to cash 11/6	0 12	6
To 1 old table cloth 3/0	0 3	0
Movables	27 2	2-1/2

Signed as greatest creditors
    John Handy
    T. Dennis

Debts due to the deceased disperate by George Jones	0 15	0
Sum totall	27 17	2-1/2

Taken on the 4th day of August 1752
[Signed by Risdon Moor, William Moor, by Nelly Collegs, John Windsor]

An Inventory of All and Singular the Goods & Chattels of Rebecca Royston Late of Calvert County Appraised this 19th Day of September 1720 by the Subscribers

	£	s.	d.
31 head of cattle	44	17	0
15 head of sheep at 6 s.	4	10	0
29 head of hogs	8	1	6
1463 lbs. tobacco at 10 s. percent	7	6	2
5 old feather bedds	16	2	0
1 flock bedd	0	10	0
Wearing apparell of the deceased	10	1	0
11 old chests and 1 box	2	6	6
1 old large seal skin trunk	0	12	0
13 old chairs and 1 old couch	1	10	0
4 old tubbs	0	13	6
9 old sickles 4 d.	0	3	0
A parcell of earthen ware and bottles	0	5	9
2 wyre 1 lawn sifter	0	6	10
4 tinn panns 1 callender 1 warming pann	0	7	6
A parcell of plantation old tools	0	12	10
A parcell of old table linning	0	5	2
1 box iron and heaters & a pair of small stillyards	0	7	0
1 old plow & old horse harness	0	7	6
1 pair of large iron doggs	0	18	0
66 lbs. of wool at 4 d. per lb. & 2 pair wool cards	1	3	4
1 bushell of salt	0	2	0
5 old casments 8 d. per	0	3	4
A parcell of old basketts	0	2	0
A parcell of old books	0	18	0
3 old candelsticks 1 flower 1 candelbox	0	1	0
2 pair tongs & fire shovels	0	3	6
50 lbs. old pewter at 7 d. & 2 new basons 1 s.	0	12	2
30 lbs. old brass at 7 d. per lb.	0	17	7
115 lbs. pott iron att 2-1/2 d. per lb.	1	2	4
1 damnified pott	0	5	0
1 pott rack 1 frying pann 1 pestle	0	5	0
1 old spitt & 1 grid iron	0	2	0
2 old gunns	0	10	0
2 pailes 2 pigens 2 bowls 1 cann 1 churn	0	6	10

	Death		185
2 old cyder casques & a parcell of lumber	2	6	0
1 old quern stone & 9 iron wedges	0	8	0
12 lbs. woolen yarn damnified at 6 d. per lb.	0	6	0
1 small looking glass	0	0	8
1 servant boy 8 years to serve	12	0	0
Sterling	114	6	8

Creditors
ISAAC JONES   GEORGE HARRIS
KENNY JONES   JOSEPH HARRIS

AN INVORY OF THE ESTATE OF
COLLNL. WM. FITZHUGH DECD

Negroes belonging to Madam Sarah Fitzhugh Relict of Colle Willm Fitzhugh

Will Black Pegg Billy her son Harry Cato Catereno Beck and Hannah. Eight in Number, Negroes belonging to Wm. Fitzhugh . . Giles Lucy, Sue, Ned, Joe, Ben, Betty Tomline and Peter. . . . 10. Negroes belonging to Henry Fitzhugh. Daphne and five Children, Caesar, Johnny Black Pegg[s] Son . . . Negroes belonging to Thomas Fitzhugh . . Mulatto Pegg her young Child Sarah and one born since named Nanny & her son George Will boy & ——Black Betty & Bettys 2 Children Harry & Frank——Negroes belonging to George Fitzhugh. Black Sarah and five Children George Jenny Moll & Cate Jenny Mulatto Sarah & her Daughter Diana[.] Negroes belonging to John Fitzhugh——Esop, Tom, Mat. Sarah Children Billy & Betsy Black Sarah Hannahs Children Clary Rose & Robin & Black Peggs son Harry—in all fivety one Negroes & Mulattoes   51

PLATE

Six silver Dishes 2 silver Basons 2 dozn. Silver Plates 4 Silver Porringers 3 Casters 3 Salvers 3 Silver Tankards 3 pair silver Candlesticks 1 small writing Do. 2 pair Snuffers & Stands 1 Silver Extinguisher 6 Silver Trencher[s] Salts 1 Table Salt 1. Dozn. Silver hafted Knifes 1 Dozen Silver Forks 1 Silver Ladle 2 Tumblers 1 Dozn. Silver Spoons 1 Silver Tobacco Box 1 Silver headed Cane 1

Silver Cork Screw 2 Silver Dishes 1 Doz: Silver Spoons 1 Bason or Bunch Bowl 1 C[h]ocolate Cup 3 Silver Salts. in all 122 pieces of Plate
  Divided between the Widow & Children as by Will. . . .

GOLD

One Gold Snuff Box two Gold Rings./Dividd. between the Widow & Exec

GOODS & MERCHANDIZES in both Stores

Five pieces & Remnants of Linnen pretty Course Quantity 115 yards—1 Remnant Jeans qt. 18 yards 1 Remnant Fustian qt. 6 yards 2 Ends Fustians 1 End Ticking qt 15 yards 1 End Do. qt. 9 yards 1 Remnant of Coloured Dimety 1 piece Striped Ditto 1 Remnant Dowlas qt. 25 yards 5 Ends of white Fustians 1 Remnt. Dowlas qt. 22 yards 1 Remnant Sacking qt. 6 yards 1 Remnant Cotton Quantity 17 yards 4 pieces Ditto 1 piece Ozimbriggs qt. 55 yards 10 pieces Course West Country Linnen 1 Remnant of the above sort qt. 21 yards 1 piece of the above Linnen qt. 55.5 pieces of Irish Linnen qt. about 105 yds 1 piece of Garlick Holland qt. 25 yards 2 Remnants of Dowlas 1 piece Course sheeting Linnen qt. 60 yards 1 Remnant Dyed Linnen 2 Bedd Tick 4 pieces of Canvis 2 pieces of Rowled Linnen 1 piece Rowled Double Canvis 27 1 piece Do. qt. 30 yds. 1 piece Rowled Canvis qt. 37 yds. 2pd. Remnts. of Dowlas 1 Remnt of Red half thick 1 Remnt. Serge 2 Remnts. of [Beys?] 5 Liverpool Coverlets abt. m 50 [sic] 8 dozn. plain shoes 2-1/2 of Mens Womens & Childrens 1 Dozn. or thereabts of Course Felts two fine Casters

HORSES & MARES

Two Mares and two Colts 1 horse called Whistler One Stone [sic] horse at the Church Quarter.

ENGLISH SERVANTS

James Jameson about 2 yrs. to serve Henry Borec 2-1/2 years to serve Thomas Barlow the same John Nicholson the same. Thomas Cave about 6-1/2 to serve Margarett an Old Woman about 2 years.

CATTLE AT HOME PLANTATION

the whole divided between the widow & Exectr. fourty four head Numberd.

SHEEP AT THE HOME PLANTAO

The whole Divided between the widow & Exec. twenty four head

HOGGS AT HOME PLANTATION

The whole divided between the widow and Executor twenty head

Cattle at the Church Quarter belonging to Henry & Thomas Fitzhugh 8 Cows 1 killed 2 heifers 3 young stears 6 Cow yearlings 4 Calves sheep being at the Church Quarter belonging to the said Henry & Thomas Fitzhugh—9 Yews & 6 Lambs Hoggs. 7 Sows Shoats & Barrons. Do 3 Breeding Sows

HOUSEHOLD FURNITURE

Henry Fitzhugh has 1 Bed of feathrs. wth. Bolster three pair sheets 1 pr. Blankets 1 Quilt 1 Pillow 1 Dozn. Napkins 1 Table Cloth Thomas Fitzhugh has 1 Bedd Bolster and Pillow 1 Blanket & Quilt 3 pair sheets 1 Dozn. Napkins & Tablecloth George Fitzhugh has 1 Bedd Bolster & Pillow 1 Blanket 1 Rugg 3 pair sheets 1 Dozn. Napkins & Table Cloth John Fitzhugh has 1 Bedd Bolster & Pillow 1 Blanket Rugg three pair sheets 1 Dozn. Napkins 1 Table Cloth The Remainder of the Household stuff to be divided between the widow & Wm. Fitzhugh the Exectr. 8 Feather Bedds Bolsters and Pillows 4 pair Blankets 2 Dozn. old leather 2 Dozn. Kaine Chairs 1 Dozn. Turkey Workt Do. 4 or 5 Tables 4 or 5 old Chests 2 Chests of Drawers 5 Standing Bedsteads 2 Truckle Ditto 2 large looking Glasses 1 Scrutore [sic] 1 small looking Glass 2 pair Brass Tongs with Shovel & Bellows 2 pair Iron Do. 4 Dozn. & 4 Napkins 2 Table Cloths 2 Leather Carpets 2 Turky work't Carpets 1 old Do. 8 pair Andirons 20 Pewter Dishes 5 Doz & 4 Pewter Plates 1 great Brass Dish 1 Copper Sistern 1 Pewter Bed Pan 1 Close Stool 4 Chafing

Dishes 1 Copper. Chocolate Pott 2 Skillets or stew pans 2 Possnets 2 stands to set Plates upon 10 Brass Candlesticks 2 Kettles 4 Iron Potts 4 Spitts 6 old Kettles 1 Brass Mortar 1 stone Do. two warming-Pans A Parcel of Pewter a parcel Tinware 1 parcel of Earthware about 2 Gross Glass Bottles a parcel of uncurryed Leather 20 pair sheets 6 Table Cloths 5 setts of Curtains and [6 allins? or Callins?] 4 Ruggs 2 Coverleds 2 Quilts 4 pair Blankets 12 Cushions 1 Iron Punch Bowl 1 Monteeth Copper Bason 1 pair Playing Tables 1 Iron Driping Pan

Cash or Ready MONEY

One Guinea one Mill Shilling Jewels unknown being in the Widows Possession together with her Apparell & Side Saddle.

A Study of Books to be divided between Wm & Henry Fitzhugh. One old Brass Clock 1 old Watch 5 old Trunk a parcel old Cask 1 Calash & Gear with 2 horses a Parcel of Rum & Sugar. Inter Partnership John Jones & Testator the Acct unsettled yet, Whenever it is there will be little coming to the Estate also About 7 £ worth Goods the 16th. part of a Ship & Cargo the Account not yet settled when ever it is shall be rendered

Wm. Fitzhugh
Henry Fitzhugh

The above Inventory presented into Court the 11th Augt. 1703 p Sworn to by Major Wm. Fitzhugh one of the Exectrs thereto subscribed

Finally, after making peace with this world, the southern colonist turned to the next. The opening lines of William Fitzhugh's will capture the religious dimension of dying in colonial Virginia. They are taken from William Fitzhugh and His Chesapeake World, *p. 373.*

In the Name of the Father Son & Holy Ghost Trinity & Unity Unity & Trinity three Persons & one God blessed for evermore Amen. I William Fitzhugh of Stafford County in the Colony of Virginia Gent being by Gods Grace bound for England and knowing the frailty & uncertainty of Mans Life and being at present in perfect health and memory do now ordain Constitute and appoint this my Last Will &

Testament Revoking all other former or other Wills this 9th. day of April 1700.

Imprimis I recomme[n]d my Soul into ye. hands of God through the mediation & Intercession of my Blessed Saviour and Redeemer hoping by the meritts of his Death and Burial to have my Sins washed away in his Blood nayled to his Cross & buryed in his grave and by his meritts and Passion to obtain everlasting Life & therefore now do dispose and Bequeath such Estate as it hath pleased God in his mercy to bestow upon me after this manner following after they have disposed my Body to decent Interment without noise feasting drink or Tumult which I not leave but injoine my Exect. or Exects. hereafter named to see decently Ex[ecuted?]